This volume of YIVO's Yiddish Voices Series was prepared for publication with generous support from the family of Harriet R. Yassky

YIVO Institute for Jewish Research

YIDDISH VOICES

Series Editors

Alyssa Quint, Yeshiva University, USA
Elissa Bemporad, Queens College and CUNY Graduate Center, USA

Yiddish Voices is an exciting new series of translated works that connects today's readers with literature that reflects the Eastern European Jewish experience, in its full range of authors, genres, and subject matter.

Published in partnership with the YIVO Institute for Jewish Research, each volume presents a rich and engaging literary work in English translation with a well-matched historian's introduction, one that is both erudite and readable. In Yiddish, the word "Yiddish" means both "Yiddish" and "Jewish"; likewise, the *Yiddish Voices* series includes translated works from an array of languages—sometimes Yiddish, but at other times Polish, Russian, or Hebrew, among others. The series thus captures both the Yiddish and the Yiddish-inflected, the Yiddish voices and Ashkenazi experiences as they came to be embedded in other cultural spheres.

Expertly curated by Alyssa Quint and Elissa Bemporad, the series is organized to showcase first-time translations of enduring texts in Yiddish from which arise topics and themes that have powerful resonance today.

Editorial Advisory Board

David Samuels, Tablet Magazine, USA
Jeffrey Shandler, Rutgers University, USA
Stefanie Halpern, Director of Collections, YIVO, USA
Barbara Kirshenblatt-Gimlet, Polin Museum, Poland
François Guesnet, University College London, UK
Joel Berkowitz, University Wisconsin, USA

Miriam Trinh, Hebrew University, Israel
Naomi Seidman, University of Toronto, Canada
Anita Norich, University of Michigan, USA

Published Titles

Three Yiddish Plays by Women: Female Jewish Perspectives, 1880–1920, ed. Alyssa Quint
The Mother of Yiddish Theatre: Memoirs of Ester-Rokhl Kaminska, ed. Mikhl Yashinsky
The Destruction of Dubova: Chronicle of a Dead City, Rokhl Faygnberg, ed. Elissa Bemporad

Upcoming Titles

Mississippi (1935) By Leyb Malakh: A Yiddish Play about the Scottsboro Boys, ed. Alyssa Quint

The Destruction of Dubova

Chronicle of a Dead City

BY ROKHL FAYGNBERG

TRANSLATED BY ALBERT MADANSKY
AND CYNTHIA MADANSKY

TRANSLATION EDITED BY
YANKL SALANT

VOLUME EDITED BY
ELISSA BEMPORAD

BLOOMSBURY ACADEMIC
LONDON • NEW YORK • OXFORD • NEW DELHI • SYDNEY

BLOOMSBURY ACADEMIC

Bloomsbury Publishing Plc, 50 Bedford Square, London, WC1B 3DP, UK
Bloomsbury Publishing Inc, 1385 Broadway, New York, NY 10018, USA
Bloomsbury Publishing Ireland, 29 Earlsfort Terrace,
Dublin 2, D02 AY28, Ireland

BLOOMSBURY, BLOOMSBURY ACADEMIC and the Diana logo are
trademarks of Bloomsbury Publishing Plc

First published in Great Britain 2025

Copyright © Elissa Bemporad, 2025

Elissa Bemporad has asserted her right under the Copyright,
Designs and Patents Act, 1988, to be identified as Editor of this work.

Cover image: The Dubova Jewish cemetery plowed over and sown with
wheat by local peasants, summer 1921. Dubova. Photograph made by
the Jewish Public Committee (Yidgezkom). © YIVO Institute. Piece of
white paper tear. © Piman Khrutmuang /Adobe Stock.

All rights reserved. No part of this publication may be: i) reproduced or
transmitted in any form, electronic or mechanical, including photocopying,
recording or by means of any information storage or retrieval system
without prior permission in writing from the publishers; or ii) used
or reproduced in any way for the training, development or operation
of artificial intelligence (AI) technologies, including generative AI
technologies. The rights holders expressly reserve this publication from
the text and data mining exception as per Article 4(3) of the Digital Single
Market Directive (EU) 2019/790.

Bloomsbury Publishing Plc does not have any control over, or
responsibility for, any third-party websites referred to or in this book.
All internet addresses given in this book were correct at the time of
going to press. The author and publisher regret any inconvenience
caused if addresses have changed or sites have ceased to exist,
but can accept no responsibility for any such changes.

A catalogue record for this book is available from the British Library.

A catalog record for this book is available from the Library of Congress.

ISBN: HB: 978-1-3505-1710-3
PB: 978-1-3505-1709-7
ePDF: 978-1-3505-1711-0
eBook: 978-1-3505-1712-7

Series: Yiddish Voices

Typeset by Integra Software Services Pvt. Ltd.
Printed and bound in Great Britain

For product safety related questions contact
productsafety@bloomsbury.com.

To find out more about our authors and books visit www.bloomsbury.com
and sign up for our newsletters.

CONTENTS

List of Figures x
List of Contributors xi

Introduction: The Story of a Text, the Voice of a Writer, the Fate of a City *Elissa Bemporad* 1

Text: Chronicle of a Dead City: The Destruction of Dubova *Rokhl Faygnberg (translated by Albert Madansky and Cynthia Madansky; translation edited by Yankl Salant)* 27

Afterword *Cynthia Madansky* 155

Notes 158

FIGURES

1 Portrait photo of Rokhl Faygnberg (1885–1972), taken in Saint Petersburg, *c.* 1910 4
2 Rokhl Faygnberg on the front page of the literary supplement to the Yiddish weekly *Der fraynd* (The Friend), July 20, 1913 6
3 Map of the Ukrainian lands controlled by the Ukrainian People's Republic, 1917–1921 8
4 Photograph of Rokhl Faygnberg and her son, early 1930s 11
5 Cover of *Chronicle of a Dead City: The Destruction of Dubova*, first published in Yiddish in Warsaw in 1926 16
6 Cover of the Russian translation of Faygnberg's *Chronicle of a Dead City*, Leningrad 1928 17
7 Photograph of the Dubova Jewish cemetery after the first pogrom, taken in 1921 20
8 Photograph of the lime pits in Dubova, taken in 1921 22

CONTRIBUTORS

Elissa Bemporad is Professor of History and Chair in East European Jewish History and the Holocaust at Queens College and the Graduate Center—CUNY. She is a two-time winner of the National Jewish Book Award. Bemporad is the author of three monographs, including *Legacy of Blood: Jews, Pogroms, and Ritual Murder in the Lands of the Soviets* (2019), and the co-editor of several volumes, including, most recently, *Pogroms: A Documentary History* (2021). Her work has appeared in different languages, including French, Hebrew, Yiddish, Italian, and Russian.

Albert Madansky (1934–2022) was a world-renowned statistician and the H.G.B. Alexander Professor Emeritus of Business Administration at University of Chicago's Booth School of Business. Dr. Madansky's parents were Jewish refugees from Poland, and he was raised with Yiddish as his first language. In addition to his academic and professional pursuits, Dr. Madansky studied and wrote about the works of Sholem Aleichem. One of his great joys during the Covid-19 pandemic was collaborating with his daughter Cynthia on this book.

Cynthia Madansky is an award-winning filmmaker and artist whose work explores cultural and political themes. Madansky has received numerous grants including the Fulbright Grant, Guggenheim Fellowship, Rome Prize, and the National Foundation for Jewish Culture. Her films have been shown at the Berlinale, Rotterdam International Film Festival, Cinema du Reél, Paris, Museum of Modern Art, the Toronto

International Film Festival, and other festivals, museums, art galleries, and community spaces.

Yankl Salant is translation editor for White Goat Press, the imprint of the Yiddish Book Center and, independently, was the translation editor and a translator for *Oyfn Sheydveg* (2023). He is, additionally, art director for the League for Yiddish and the graphic designer of a majority of its publications. Salant also specializes in translating handwritten documents from Yiddish to English, Spanish, and Italian. An associate editor of the *Comprehensive Yiddish-English Dictionary* (2013), he was bibliographic editor and a translator for the *YIVO Encyclopedia of Jews in Eastern Europe* (2008).

Introduction

The Story of a Text, the Voice of a Writer, the Fate of a City

Elissa Bemporad

On Tuesday, October 18, 1927, in a packed room in the Court of Assizes in Paris, the principal criminal court in France, a sensational trial against a young Ukrainian Jew shook the world. The defendant in the trial, which lasted for eight days, until October 26, was Sholem Schwarzbard. Born in Izmail, a port city about 120 miles west of Odesa, Schwarzbard took part in the Russian Revolution of 1905 as a supporter of anarchism, then moved to France and settled in Paris where he made a living as a watchmaker. In the early afternoon of May 25, 1926, in the heart of the Parisian Latin Quarter, at the corner of Rue Racine and Boulevard Saint-Michel, Schwarzbard shot, in cold blood, Symon Petliura, the president of the Directory (equivalent of the cabinet) of the Ukrainian People's Republic, and, at the time, head of the Ukrainian government-in-exile in the French capital.[1] Petliura had relocated to Paris in 1924, after fleeing the victorious Red Army that held sway over most of the territories of the former Russian Empire on behalf of Soviet power. As Schwarzbard openly admitted to the police who arrested him, to the judges who tried him one year after the murder, and to the hundreds of spectators who listened intently in the Paris courtroom, he had assassinated the leader of the Ukrainian army deliberately. Schwarzbard held Petliura personally responsible for the death of thousands of Jewish men, women, and children, who were murdered between 1918 and 1921 during the bloody civil war that consumed the eastern territories of the European continent after the Bolshevik Revolution. As many as 150,000 Jews were murdered. Scores of pogroms were carried out by the Ukrainian forces under the leadership of Petliura.[2] The victims of the mass violence, some of the most devastating in the centuries-long history of East European Jews, included twelve members of Schwarzbard's family.

The world paid careful attention to Schwarzbard's trial. *Time* magazine described it as "one of the most gruesome, bloodcurdling, impassioned trials ever to be held in that vaulted hall of justice."[3] The American weekly vividly (and condescendingly deploying more than one ethnic stereotype) captured the mood surrounding the trial: "Quivering flappers sat to gasp with astonishment beside white and black bearded Jews who exchanged shocked glances with flat-faced Slavic Ukrainians under the noses of red and black-robed judges. Within and without the courtroom was a triple guard of gendarmes to prevent disorder."[4] Across the Jewish world, newspapers, but also political activists, and charitable organizations from as far as Argentina, Australia, and Tunisia, gave rise to a global effort to collect funds and gather the voices of witnesses to support Schwarzbard's defense.[5] In October 1927, Schwarzbard was acquitted.

In his impassioned address, defense attorney Henri Torres, one of France's leading criminal lawyers, won over the jury by arguing that the trial was not about adjudicating Schwarzbard's fate, but rather about the horror of pogrom violence.[6] Torres built his argument drawing from a vast trove of evidence, the bulk of which had been collected and submitted to the defense by the Schwarzbard Defense Committee. Established shortly after the assassination and made up of prominent Jewish intellectuals and activists living in France at the time, including writers, jurists, and historians, one of the organization's key purposes was "preparing all materials about the Jewish pogroms in Ukraine and about the role that Petliura played in those pogroms ..."[7] If the twelve members of the jury in the Court of Assizes returned a verdict of not guilty for Sholem Schwarzbard, it was, to a large extent, thanks to the eyewitness testimonies by survivors and the written accounts of devastation and suffering assembled by the Defense Committee.

One of these texts was Rokhl Faygnberg's *Chronicle of a Dead City: The Destruction of Dubova*, reproduced here in English for the first time. Originally written in Yiddish and translated into French at the time of the trial to corroborate Petliura's responsibility for the crimes, *Chronicle of a Dead City* is a harrowing account of life and death in the small market-town (shtetl) of Dubova, located thirteen miles southeast of the city of Uman, in the Cherkasy region, in central Ukraine. The pogroms essentially wiped Dubova off the map along with its Jewish inhabitants.[8] Before we dive into the text itself and dissect its unique literary and historical features, we will pause and discuss its author, her life experience, and what drove her to craft such a powerful tale of obliteration.

* * *

Rokhl Faygnberg was born in 1885 in the tiny shtetl of Liuban, located midway between the cities of Vilna (Vilnius) and Minsk, in the heartland of Lita.[9] She grew up in a religious family, gripped by poverty. Her grandfather was the shtetl's rabbi, and her father, steeped in the study of Kabbalah, made a living as a melamed, a teacher in a traditional elementary school, while her mother, who ran a small shop, bequeathed to her daughter a profound devotion to religion and prayer.[10] Perhaps because her grandfather was a rabbi, young Faygnberg joined the shtetl's wealthy family's children to study Hebrew, Yiddish, and Russian with a private tutor.[11] As for many women at the time, her path to becoming a writer was far from easy. It was hindered by the family's financial difficulties, made more dire when her mother's illness forced her to interrupt her studies and take care of the shop. Soon, the early loss of both parents forced her to fend for herself.

Faygnberg's aspirations to write were also curbed by the cultural bigotries embedded in the shtetl's patriarchal society. When at the age of thirteen she penned her first novel

FIGURE 1 *Portrait photo of Rokhl Faygnberg (1885–1972) taken in Saint Petersburg, where she temporarily lived to take university courses toward a pedagogical degree that she never completed, c. 1910. Courtesy of Daphna Levy, the granddaughter of Faygnberg.*

Yoysef un Roza (Joseph and Rosa), which was inspired by the wondrous stories of rabbis and tsaddikim that her grandmother gifted to her, but also by the works of fiction of the popular Yiddish writer Shomer,[12] Faygnberg ended up burning the manuscript. The scandal that erupted after her family discovered the manuscript was too overwhelming.[13]

At fifteen, following her mother's death, Faygnberg moved to Odesa and worked as a seamstress in the garment industry for four years; despite the harsh work conditions, during the day she entertained her coworkers by retelling them stories from Russian literature that she had read at night. Faygnberg first emerged on the literary scene in 1905, when her work *Kinderyorn* (Childhood Years), an autobiographical account of shtetl life, appeared in the Yiddish monthly *Dos lebn* (Life).[14] Her realistic and earnest portrayal of shtetl society together with her simple and immediate Yiddish, yielded positive reviews. After temporarily moving first to Saint Petersburg and then to Lausanne, Switzerland, to take university courses toward a pedagogical degree that she never completed, Faygnberg gave up her studies and returned to Ukraine (then under the Russian Empire) due to precarious material circumstances.[15] Here, driven both by her creative ethos and the necessity to make ends meet, she put her pen to work and crafted short sketches and novels, which appeared in some of the major Yiddish publications at the time, including *Der fraynd* (The Friend) and *Haynt* (Today).

Faygnberg became the first professional Jewish female author who earned a living from writing novels and penning essays for the Yiddish and Hebrew press.[16] In and alongside her fiction, including autobiographical fiction, her work touches upon a panoply of momentous events that reshaped the territories of the Russian Empire and of the Jewish communities within its confines. Because she witnessed so many turning points in twentieth-century Jewish history—including revolutions, wars, pogroms, refugee crises, and the establishment of the State of Israel—Yiddish writer and cultural activist Melech Ravitch described her life as "the biography of an era."[17]

FIGURE 2 *Rokhl Faygnberg on the front page of the literary supplement to the Yiddish weekly* Der fraynd *(The Friend) to celebrate the paper's tenth anniversary. Dated July 20, 1913. A different writer was portrayed on the front page of each weekly issue through the year. All are men, save for Faygnberg and writer Sore Rejzen. Courtesy of David Mazower.*

***

In 1914, on the eve of the First World War, Faygnberg married and settled in Yanokva (or Yanivka, now Bereslavka), a small shtetl near Odesa located on the road that led to the city of Balta. Here, she set aside her pen and, for five years, devoted herself to the quite shtetl life.[18] "My family responsibilities kept me away from literature and literary circles," she wrote, explaining why she interrupted the writer's vagabond life. As she told her close friend and mentor Mordkhe Spektor, a prominent writer and editor, and the author of more than a dozen novels and short stories in Yiddish, "I have finally become a housewife like any other ... I traded my pen for the soup ladle!"[19] And when Spektor encouraged her to write a short piece for a literary collection that he was working on, she retorted, hinting at how the practicality of married life took a toll on her literary creativity, "... what kind of writer am I now? How can I now find the time for such things? The Jewish holidays are almost here, then I have to prepare some food for the winter, I need to marinate the squash, pickle the tomatoes, cook the preserves and jams ..."[20] While she promised him she would write her housewife story, she never did. Only the extraordinary events of war and revolution would pull the ordinary domesticity of Faygnberg's life—and the lives of so many others—into a vortex of unimaginable destruction and death. They would also return her to her writing table.

The First World War and the two Russian Revolutions of 1917 (the democratic revolution of February that prompted Tsar Nicholas II's abdication, and the Bolshevik coup of October with Lenin's storming of the Winter Palace) paved the way to a bloody civil war. From 1918 through 1922 the war engulfed the territories of present-day Ukraine, Belarus, and Southern Russia, and involved different armies and military forces. While the Red Army waged a war for the victory of Bolshevism, vying to control the territory of the former Tsarist Empire, the White movement, under the leadership of General Anton Denikin, fought for the return of autocracy to the lands of the Russian Empire and the defeat of Soviet power. The Ukrainian army fought to retain the coveted independence of the Ukrainian People's Republic, which was established in December 1917, fending off pro-Bolshevik forces. At the same time, while fighting on behalf of the recently established Second Polish Republic, Polish troops faced the Red Army from early 1919 until 1921, as a diverse group of anarchist peasant bands, whose ideological position fluctuated between supporting the Bolsheviks and disassociating themselves from the ideology of the other combatants, also took part in the war. All troops and military units perpetrated atrocities against the Jewish population, with thousands of civilians participating in the violence and looting, often swayed by old and new antisemitic prejudices as well as by the desperate socio-economic conditions exacerbated by the war. Unlike the previous waves of pogroms that had swept through the Jewish communities living under the Tsar in 1881–1882, in 1903, and in 1905–1906, these pogroms resulted from a deadly and

FIGURE 3 *Map of the Ukrainian lands controlled by the Ukrainian People's Republic, 1917–1921. The borders shifted over the course of the civil war as the troops fighting on behalf of the Ukrainian national movement and the Directory faced the Red Army, the White Volunteer Army, and the Second Polish Republic troops. Besides major Ukrainian cities, such as Kharkiv and Kyiv, shown by circles with a dot, the map also includes the smaller towns that are either mentioned in* Chronicle of a Dead City *or relate to Fayngberg's biography. Courtesy of Yankl Salant.*

unprecedented combination of military actions and neighbor-on-neighbor violence. The enormity and catastrophic nature of the violence, its unprecedented brutality and scale, marked a rupture in the long history of pogroms in the territories of the Russian Empire.[21] What ensued then constituted the worst episode of anti-Jewish violence in modern history before the Holocaust.

The motivation for the violence differed vastly, but was often rooted in anti-Jewish stereotypes. The economic collapse engendered by war since 1914 egged on soldiers and local peasants to plunder the "Jewish capitalists" and exploiters of the proletariat. On the other hand, the exclusivist nationalism that peaked during the First World War encouraged political leaders and military personnel on all sides to label the Jewish minority as disloyal and treacherous toward the Ukrainian dream of nationhood, the Polish reestablished nation-state, and the Russian vision of revitalized empire.[22] In the midst of a fierce war over land and political sovereignty, the troops and civilian population often imagined the Jews as compromised political actors that spread communism and tore at the heart of the nation's fabric, often notwithstanding their actual political choice.[23] The civil war served as a fertile ground for the lie of Judeo-Bolshevism; the myth that communism was a Jewish plot to destroy other nations served as a prime justification to attack the Jewish communities.[24]

The Ukrainian lands became the main stage of the battlefront. Here, where all forces clashed in combat, and where one of the largest Jewish communities in Europe had lived and thrived for centuries, generating a unique diversity of religious, political, and cultural identities, the brutality of war hit the hardest. Approximately 1,500 pogroms, which resulted in murder, rape, and systematic pillaging, were carried out in more than eight hundred towns and shtetls, most of them located in Ukraine in the territories to the west of Kyiv and along the River Dnipro. The shtetl Yanovka—where Faygnberg had been living with her newborn son on the eve of the violence—was located here; as was the shtetl Dubova—the erasure of which she would chronicle in the account that the defense presented to the jury in the Schwarzbard trial.

The terror Faygnberg witnessed, experienced, and survived profoundly influenced her work and life. In the summer of 1919, at the height of the Jewish massacres, when her "fine small-town home with its acacia trees below its windows was destroyed," she went into hiding among the peasants in nearby villages, "holding my child in my arms." Her husband—and the father of her child—had died at the beginning at the civil war. She was alone. At the risk of death, she eventually managed to reach Odesa, but only after concealing her identity:

> a good-hearted Bulgarian peasant gave me her holiday dress with the national colors for the journey, and I put a little cross around my child's neck ... not only were Jew-murderers still roaming around the Balta roads, but signposts ... were still hanging from the telephone poles, calling on people to kill all little Jewish boys, because when they grow up they will all be communists ...[25]

Homeless and traumatized by violence and dispossession, Faygnberg still heeded the writer's calling. Equipped with a pencil and a notebook, she began daily visits to the building of the Odesa Jewish community, where hundreds of refugees came together, and recorded the horror stories of those who had fled their shtetls, and of those whose families had been murdered.[26] These were stories of extreme and pervasive violence, cruelty, and suffering. To be sure, many Jewish intellectuals, writers, doctors, and activists at the time tried to make sense of the violence, by documenting it, recording it, and memorializing it through the written word. Some writers produced forms of documentary fiction. Others wrote poetry. Physicians and aid workers collected evidence of sexual violence against Jewish girls and women, showing how rape had reached massive proportions, and no longer lay at the periphery of violence but at its heart.[27] Compared to men, women may have been too burdened by the immediate practical needs of everyday life

FIGURE 4 *Photograph of Rokhl Faygnberg and her son, who at the time of the pogroms was less than a year old. She fled the massacres of 1919 by going into hiding with her son among local peasants. After spending some time in Kishinev, Bucharest, Warsaw, and Paris, they eventually settled in Mandate Palestine. The photograph was taken in the early 1930s in Tel Aviv. Courtesy of Daphna Levy, the granddaughter of Faygnberg.*

that followed destruction to turn to writing: assuming that they would be the primary target of violence, many husbands and fathers fled as the invading troops approached, leaving behind wives and daughters to look after the children. Despite all this, some women managed to respond to the violence by compiling historical and literary accounts of the pogroms. Faygnberg emerged as one of the most powerful female chroniclers of the genocidal violence of the civil war, or of the *khurbn*, as the destruction of Ukrainian Jewry came to be known at the time.[28] Her work belongs to what Laura Jockusch has called "*khurbn-forshung*," or "destruction research," a unique genre of popular history writing that emerged in response to the First World War and the anti-Jewish violence of the civil war.[29]

Faygnberg later recalled the words of her friend, the writer and editor Mordkhe Spektor, who encouraged her to chronicle the destruction: "everything must be recorded."[30] She might also have been inspired by the deeds of the great historian Elias Tcherikower, who dedicated most of his life to the meticulous collection and recording of the pogroms of this period. He defined the anti-Jewish violence unleashed during the civil war as "one of the worse catastrophes that has ever shaken the fate of the greatest Jewish center in the world ... which was devastated, shattered into pieces, and broken to its economic foundation."[31] Upon learning about Faygnberg's interviews with survivors, Tcherikower assigned her the task of chronicling the destruction of a number of small Jewish settlements: after all, the Ukrainian shtetl, pillaged by different troops and peasant insurgent groups, was at the center of the massacres. Because she was intimately acquainted with shtetl life and its Jews, who constituted the demographic group mostly affected by the violence, Faygnberg seemed the ideal person for the task. She thus became the only woman to collaborate with Tcherikower (besides his wife Riva) in the creation of a unique archive of data and witness accounts about the Jewish fate during the civil war. One of the accounts she produced in the wake of the violence, which, in summer 1922 she sent to Berlin, where Tcherikower had relocated together with his archive, describes the destruction of Dubova.[32]

***

Faygnberg wrote two accounts of the destruction of Dubova. This first one is a shorter reportage of devastation, and was written between the end of 1921 and the early months of 1922. The second and expanded version, on which she worked over the course of the next few years, appeared in book form in 1926 and is reproduced in English in this volume. Both versions are based on the witness testimonies that Faygnberg collected while interviewing survivors in Odesa, as well as on the data and photographs of victims, destroyed property, and mass graves she obtained from the local branch of the Jewish Committee to Aid the Victims of the Pogroms.[33] Both versions of the account share the same title: *Pinkes fun a toyter shtot: khurbn Dubove*, or *Chronicle of a Dead City: The Destruction of Dubova*. The term *pinkes*, or chronicle, refers to the register or book of records that the Jewish communities of Eastern Europe traditionally used to record noteworthy or unusual events relating to the community's life. These comprised occasions from the community's everyday life, such as marriages, births, and deaths, as well as extraordinary events like natural disasters or wars that may have affected Jewish property, including synagogues and cemeteries. In Faygnberg's account the term evokes the idea of a register of death of the community. Each date is recorded according to the Hebrew calendar. Whether it was to commemorate precisely when Jews were killed, this choice makes it into an inherently Jewish account, inscribed into a Jewish calendar, embedded in Jewish religious practice and culture.

The words "dead city" in the title evoke one of the most influential texts in the Jewish canon, namely Hayim Nahman Bialik's poem "In the City of Killing," written in Hebrew in the summer of 1903 after the poet spent five weeks interviewing witnesses to the Kishinev pogrom. If the city of Kishinev, where forty-nine Jews were murdered in April 1903, became in Bialik's poem the "city of killing," Dubova, which in 1919 experienced the complete elimination of its Jews and their history, became in Faygnberg's account a "dead city."[34] Bialik's poem may have figured even more significantly as inspiration for Faygnberg because of the time she spent in Kishinev, after fleeing the Ukrainian lands in late 1921 and crossing the border into Bessarabia.³⁵ Bialik's literary rendering of the Kishinev massacre likely came to mind as she began to write down what she had seen and what she had heard. She was looking for a historical analogy in times of crisis. The use of the term "dead city" furthermore emphasizes the intense bonds between East European Jewish communities and the places in which they resided; by anthropomorphizing the town itself, the term turned it into the main character in the story, who died together with its residents.

With the word *khurbn* in the title, Faygnberg connected the destruction of Dubova to a longer chain of catastrophes in Jewish history, from the destruction in Jerusalem of the First Temple in 586 BCE and the Second Temple in 70 CE, through the devastation of the crusades, expulsions, blood libels, and the exclusionary anti-Jewish violence on the Eastern Front during the First World War. She thus inscribed the obliteration of Dubova into the Jewish collective memory of persecution and destruction, adding her voice to the well-established Jewish literary tradition of responding to catastrophe.³⁶

In the account's first version, Faygnberg's writing seemed prompted primarily by a strong sense of urgency to report the bloody events, to remember its victims, and to incriminate the perpetrators. In fact, this initial account, made up of twenty-six typed pages, addresses all but nothing about life in Dubova before 1919. Time almost stands still. It is marked by the year of the massacres only, so that everything begins and ends in 1919. What takes center stage in this first account is the sheer brutality of the killing and the tremendous loss of life, which Faygnberg conveys by incorporating necrologies, or lists of those who died, inclusive of the name, age, and profession of the victim. This practice echoes the medieval genre started by Isaac ben Samuel of Meningen who in his 1296 *Memorbuch* recorded the Jewish communities destroyed and the individuals killed in Northern Europe at the time of the Crusades.³⁷ In closing the first version of her account, Faygnberg avowed the following:

I, Rokhl Faygnberg, collected and recorded this account in the winter of 1921. The twelve homeless families from Dubova who fled to Odesa compiled the lists of the victims. The lists do not include those who drowned in the river, those who were lost in the woods and on the roads and paths and the children who died of hunger in the fields where they were fed the grains from the green ears of corn. Nobody can remember them. Nobody can say when, where and how many of them died.[38]

Over the course of the following three years, while living between Bucharest, Warsaw, Paris, and Mandate Palestine, Faygnberg worked on the second and expanded version of the account of Dubova's destruction. In a way, the new version, which was published as a book in 1926, and used as evidence of Petliura's crimes in the Schwarzbard trial, represented an attempt to counter her own original statement of "nobody can remember them." In other words, the newer version of *Chronicle of a Dead City* constituted Faygnberg's response to history's excision of Dubova from memory. It was still a *pinkes*, or the community's record book. But this time it also recorded the life of the community, before its devastation. It became the only vestige of the Dubova community. It resulted from the writer's effort to chronicle not only the shtetl's death, but its life too, rescuing it and its inhabitants from oblivion, and making sure that a record of the past was not lost. Faygnberg felt the imperative to capture the shtetl's life in all its fullness. She knew the community's devastation meant something different when measured against the texture of its life. By doing so, Faygnberg inserted her account into a library of catastrophe, anticipating the Jewish commemorative genre of the *yizker bikher*, or memorial books, which were published in large numbers after the Holocaust to document Jewish life in the different towns and cities in Eastern Europe affected by the Second World War before the genocide.[39]

Somehow then, Faygnberg—the survivor, the essayist, and the novelist—took on the role of historian too: she established that such a place had once existed in order to preserve its memory. She thus turned her written word into a kind of monument to the destroyed town and its inhabitants, as captured in the image of a tombstone with the town's name on the book's cover.

FIGURE 5 *Cover of* Chronicle of a Dead City: The Destruction of Dubova, *first published in Yiddish in Warsaw in 1926. On the background of ruins of destroyed homes and shattered windows, a large tombstone appears, on which the shtetl's name is inscribed in Yiddish. At the top of the page the words "Khurbn Dubove" (The Destruction of Dubova) bleed onto the tombstone.*

FIGURE 6 *Cover of the Russian translation of Faygnberg's* Chronicle of a Dead City, *which appeared in Leningrad in 1928, translated by the prominent cultural historian Saul Ginzburg. On the cover a hole in a red brick wall opens up onto a dark and cloudy night that hovers over the ruins of the destroyed shtetl.*

***

First published in Yiddish, in Warsaw, in 1926 (with French and Russian versions that appeared respectively in 1927 and 1928), *Chronicle of a Dead City: The Destruction of Dubova* starts out with a detailed portrayal of life in the shtetl.[40] Faygnberg appears as both an outsider/omniscient writer and an insider/eyewitness to the very events she describes (and in many ways had experienced herself). She introduces the readers to the ebb and flow of everyday life of the Jewish community of Dubova. A community that dated back to the late eighteenth century and that never rose to the greatness of a renowned center of rabbinic learning or Hasidism, nor one of noteworthy modern cultural or political Jewish enterprises. She records the virtuous and less virtuous deeds of the town's Jewish residents, with their petty passions, emotions, dreams, tensions, and who, together with their institutions, lived at the center of the town, surrounded by Ukrainian villages and lavish forests.[41] Unlike other examples in the Jewish memorial canon, including, for instance, Natan Hannover's account of the destruction of the Jewish communities at the time of the 1648 Khmelnytsky uprising, or of many of the *yizker bikher* that appeared after 1945, Faygnberg's portrayal is devoid of nostalgia and never romanticizes or idealizes the shtetl inhabitants.[42] She acknowledges their ordinariness: they never produced a particularly novel or sophisticated expression of Jewish culture. Traces of modern secular culture and politics had penetrated the life of the shtetl, Zionism and the Ukrainian national cause, most significantly. Mostly, however, Jewish life revolved around the traditional elementary school, the heder, Dubova's two main synagogues, and a yeshiva for its most talented students. The shtetl's rabbi, Moshe Arn Berdyczewski, father of the well-known Hebrew writer Micha Yosef Berdyczewski, spent his days studying, aloof from the practical matters of everyday life, while his wife supported the family through the monopoly to sell yeast. She also baked the traditional challah bread for the shtetl widows and orphans with flour provided by the town's bread merchants.[43]

From the beginning, Faygnberg tells us that the shtetl never operated as an entirely Jewish world. Unsurprisingly, the lives of Jews and their neighbors were closely intertwined, harmonious even, until the war broke out, as Jews and peasants tended to need each other economically.[44] On Thursdays peasants from surrounding villages would bring in their grain, Jews would buy it, mill the grain, and then sell the flour in Uman and in other places. The First World War and the Revolution altered the economic equilibrium that existed in the shtetl: bread turned instantly into gold, and tensions over speculation and black marketing grew exponentially. Capturing the richness of life in the shtetl, Faygnberg introduced to the reader those Jews who espoused the Ukrainian cause (without concealing her resentment for them), including the pharmacist and his wife, who had settled in Dubova from Uman and felt self-conscious about their Jewishness, or the beautiful nieces of the mill owner Shkodnik, who only spoke Ukrainian, hung out with the Ukrainian youth, and were fond of Ukrainian folk songs.

Besides masterfully opening a window onto everyday life in a shtetl caught up in the earth-shattering events of war, terror, and revolution, the power of Faygnberg's account lies in her ability to capture the different times of the pogrom, the time to live and the time to die. The pogrom upset preexisting notions of time that marked the quotidian in times of peace. To be sure, the slow pace of life in the shtetl, a time that almost seemed to flow backwards, had been disrupted in many places as early as 1915, with the inception of the First World War, when thousands of Jews, branded as "enemy others" and identified as a liability for Russia's national security, faced sudden and violent mass deportations. But the years of the civil war brought about a new degree of intensity in the fast-changing pace of time.

Over the course of twelve months, beginning in mid-1918, Dubova came under the command successively of each of the forces involved in the conflict, including the Red Army, the White Volunteer Army, the troops loyal to Symon Petliura's Directory, and diverse groups of armed peasant bands whose political allegiances vacillated inconsistently according to the needs of the day. The major players committing massacres in Dubova included the soldiers fighting on behalf of Denikin's White Army, and the military forces under Petliura's command. In both cases, Ukrainian peasants and bandits took part in the looting and murder of their neighbors. This whirlwind of violence took on the "speed of cinematography." The secular time of politics and military actions became the time of violence, unsettling Dubova's Jewish inhabitants: "[A]fterward they sat by the locked doors and gates and listened to every sound. In the quiet one could hear their hearts beating. The shtetl clocks broke the dead silence, counting the hours in the endless interval waiting for something dreadful." The secular time of military actions and violence interrupted the rhythmical flow of everyday life, which was measured by the Jewish calendar, the Hebrew dates, the customs, the holidays, the religious practice: "Until Tisha b'Av the people in Dubova were comforted by this sweet bright hope ..."[45]

Three main pogroms succeeded each other from May to August 1919, with the "small massacre" first, a display of intimate violence carried out mostly by local peasants who, following the Bolsheviks' retreat from the shtetl, attacked

FIGURE 7 *Photograph of the Dubova Jewish cemetery after the first pogrom, which took place in mid-May 1919, on the eve of Shavuot. The victims of the first pogrom lie in a mass grave under the overturned tombstone. Photograph was taken in 1921. Courtesy of the Archives of the YIVO Institute for Jewish Research, New York.*

their Jewish neighbors with pitchforks and axes, but not before having smeared their faces so that they would not be recognized by their neighbors. The carnage became vindictive, as when the peasant Kirilo Tsherniuk "[k]illed the girl Sonye Shoshkin in the garden of one of his neighbors ... She had hidden herself in the peasant gardens where she encountered Kirilo who shot her in the head. Wounded, she ran into the river, but he dragged her out and back to the garden and hacked off a few of her limbs ..." The second pogrom, referred to as "the silent massacre," lasted four days, and was accompanied by extensive destruction and looting, triggered by the critical loss of economic stability by all social classes in and about town: the second time around the perpetrators carried out the massacres under the slogan of "more dead!"

The third time around, the violence intensified further. The pogrom, referred to by survivors as the "Great Massacre," was carried out in early August 1919 by insurgent forces, mostly loyal to Petliura, who fought against the Red Army, with hundreds of Jews murdered at the site of the lime pits. The violence became more public, it became ritualized, even carnivalesque and turned into a sort of circus drawing the bystanders' curious eyes. It included the public spectacle of mass rape, which became more pervasive once looting was no longer an option and nothing else of value was left to take; mass rape occurred in two-thirds of the pogroms and thousands of Ukrainian Jewish women and girls became victims of sexual violence. Faygnberg captures the everydayness of rape, eerily intertwined with the flow of time and the colors and sounds of nature: "This is how the day passed. The heat was great, and in the surrounding sunny golden fields they were cutting the ripe grain, and along with this, the screaming of those being raped and tortured to death split the bright blue skies..."; "These human-beasts already had their fill of slaughters and murders. They were still dragging girls and women off to be raped. They tore off the dirty bonnets and kerchiefs from the dark and blonde heads of those who were made-up and disguised as old women, but they no longer took their souls."

FIGURE 8 *Photograph of the lime pits, where the perpetrators buried the corpses of the victims of the third pogrom (some of whom were buried alive), thus robbing them of burial rites and individual graves. As stated on the back of the photo the individuals portrayed in the photograph have no relation to the photograph itself. Faygnberg obtained the photograph from the local branch of the Jewish Committee to Aid the Victims of the Pogroms, which collected data and took photographs of victims, of destroyed property and mass graves. Photograph was taken in 1921. Courtesy of the Archives of the YIVO Institute for Jewish Research, New York.*

In due course, the perpetrators not only killed nearly the entire community of Jews, but proceeded to destroy important symbols of Jewish life. They destroyed, for instance, the Jewish cemetery, along with the gravestones, plowing through it, and planting it with grain, fields, and gardens, thereby removing the "place and consciousness of Jewish Dubova." They excised the very memory of Jewish Dubova, removing or erasing, in a way, the time when Jews had lived there. If the Jews had never lived there, then the crimes against them had never occurred.

One of the chronicle's strongest features is that it renders this catastrophe at a human level, it allows the reader to grasp its magnitude through the experience of the inhabitants of a single town. Faygnberg's account humanizes the victims, recreating in real time their fears, their despair, their vulnerability, their powerlessness: "Everything was packed up. Everything was ready for flight. There was an air of desolation. At night they slept in their clothes, all their relatives and friends gathered under one roof, and the day frightened them with pain and misery. A depression fell upon them, the news from everywhere made them insane. There was nowhere to run." She narrates the complicated political and military events of the war through the lives of the town's residents, both its anti-heroes—like the lawyer Nestrovsky, who wore his conversion certificate around his neck like a lucky charm—and its heroes—like Moyshe the wheelwright, who attempted to resist obliteration, extracting the bodies from the lime pits and burying them in the Jewish cemetery.[46]

The utter chaos of the civil war is thus conveyed through the townspeople's microcosm, and encompassed by the sounds, emotions, and time of the violence. Time determined the victims' response to the violence; there was a window of time during which victims could express their agency in the midst of violence, during which it was still possible to build a secret hiding place unbeknownst to one's neighbors; during which it was still possible to hope to elude the possibility of death by converting to Christianity; during which it was still possible to flee the shtetl under attack and reach the nearby town's self-defense unit.[47] The power of rumors enveloped the hearts of those fleeing ("Someone who fled from Uman said that America had sent an army to save the Jews of Ukraine"); naivete and folk-beliefs muddled the response to violence by some of the victims ("Whenever a gang would storm in, young and old would run to the rabbi's home. Whoever managed to fit inside was certain that they would remain alive because of the rabbi's virtue"); while others attempted to come up with rational solutions, building ingenious secret hiding places and dug-outs, digging at night for weeks, constructing complicated airshaft system and light, until the crying baby gave away their hideout.

The microcosm of violence is rich with ambivalences too. When chronicling the violence, Faygnberg's words shed light on the sudden moment when friendly relations break down, when genocidal impulses supersede peaceful coexistence, leading neighbors to mock, torture, and kill. The factors that sparked the violence at the local level included the tensions of the war years from 1915–1917, the unsettling presence of outside armies, the surge of Ukrainian nationalism, which for many seemed an answer to all setbacks, and the contradictory views on antisemitism, ranging from the widespread belief in Jews' responsibility for the economic crisis to conspiracies of Jewish power, exploited in particular to make sense of Bolshevism (one perpetrator explicitly stated that they had to kill Jewish boys because "once they grew up, they would all become communists"). But if Faygnberg captures the moment when pogrom violence turns intimate or familiar, and is carried out by fellow townspeople outside of the realm of organized military violence, she also captures the unexpected moment when friendly relations are restored; when neighbors suddenly become rescuers and guardians, and offer the victims a refuge, as "the old peasant who let everyone into his orchard ... and fed the Jewish boys and girls hidden in the garden."

Gender played an important role in dictating the suspension of violence and in repairing neighborly attitudes and relations at the time of the pogroms. Neighbors offered support and care, albeit not to everyone. As in other genocidal contexts in different times and places, gender defined the refugee experience: disguising one's identity, converting to Russian Orthodoxy as a measure to shun the violence, or hiding among neighbors may have been easier for Jewish women than it was for men. A Ukrainian neighbor offered safety to many Jewish women and children who survived the three pogroms carried out in the shtetl. In exchange for furniture and personal objects of value, he allowed the widows and orphans to hide in his home ("... the Jewish widows and orphans were entirely under the protection of Dimitri Shabolinski. Not for nothing was Shabolinski called 'the zhid father' in the Gentile streets").[48]

***

Faygnberg's chronicle of Dubova—one that describes a set of events that unfolded in different iterations in many Jewish settlements throughout the Ukrainian lands during this period—reminds us that the shtetl in Eastern Europe was not obliterated by the Nazis alone. Over the course of the 1920s and 1930s, the Bolsheviks forcibly and violently Sovietized society, including those regions in Ukraine west of the River Dnipro. This process entailed, among other things, liquidating bourgeois and nationalist institutions, bringing down existing economic infrastructures, uprooting religious practices, and transforming men, women, and children into loyal Soviet citizens. As a result, many shtetls ceased to exist as historical-sociological and cultural entities long before 1941, when the Germans launched their attack on the Soviet Union and annihilated hundreds of thousands of its Jewish residents.[49] In many cases, even these destructive forces were preempted by the pogromist violence that Faygnberg describes. By the fall of 1920, for instance, there were no more Jews living in Dubova, which meant that the Soviets did not have to deracinate prerevolutionary Jewish life, and that the Germans and their collaborators did not have to exterminate its Jewish population in 1941–1942.[50]

Faygnberg never visited Dubova after the pogroms. Nor did she ever return to her shtetl located between Balta and Odesa—there was nothing to return to. Like thousands of other refugees, she left the region for good and participated in one of the greatest demographic revolutions in modern Jewish history: emigration abroad. After reaching the Romanian border, and making her way into Poland, where she lived for some time, she eventually settled in Mandate Palestine.[51] Leaving the cities of death did not relinquish the memory of the pogroms; their memory resurfaced with renewed power during the Second World War, when in 1940 she translated *Chronicle of a Dead City* into Hebrew.[52] The events of the Second World War must have taken her back to 1919. Yet this book, together with the pogroms it chronicles, and the numerous documents and witness testimonies assembled in the archives and in the reports penned by historians, journalists, and poets, were soon forgotten and eclipsed by the Holocaust. Reading it reminds us then of a largely neglected chapter in European history and in the history of mass violence against Jews. Reading *Chronicle of a Dead City* allows us to scan the many complexities of the forgotten violence of the civil war, overshadowed because it took place in the same territories that twenty years later became the epicenter of the genocide of European Jewry. At the intersection of different genres, including history, literature, chronicle, Jewish memorial literature, and "*khurbn-forshung*," Faygnberg's account presages later scholarship on genocide, which we know kills more than just people. It discloses for us the tenuous interplay between ruptures and continuities in modern ethnic violence, the tension between the politics and memory of mass violence, and the unexpected ways in which violence can sway the emotions and behaviors of neighbors.

The reader of the following pages might be surprised at first by a prose that describes a litany of gruesome and horrific atrocities, enumerated in a detailed and detached fashion, without imposing artistic value. The ensuing horror story is almost entirely unmediated by narrative or literary style. This is, however, a reminder that the key importance of Rokhl Faygnberg's chronicle is not its literary merit but rather the work it does in documenting history and recovering memory. For us readers, Faygnberg memorializes the obliterated shtetl Dubova, rescuing its Jewish past from the total erasure from the landscape of Ukraine.

Text
Chronicle of a Dead City: The Destruction of Dubova

Rokhl Faygnberg

Translated by Albert Madansky and Cynthia Madansky

Translation edited by Yankl Salant

1

In olden times Dubova (Дубово) was a Polish noble estate, part of the Podvisote fiefdom.[1] It comprised twelve villages encircled by a forest of old oak trees, lush, green meadows, and blessed fields of grain that belonged to the Tshetvertinsky dukes. Afterward the tract was the property of the noblemen of Korzhova. Thereafter the estates of the Podvisote fiefdom were sold piece by piece, and the Dubova tract was purchased by Radokanaki the Greek. From him Dubova was turned over to the well-established Russian Durilin. Those last years

Dubova remained quite a small estate, as Radokanaki had sold the land around the shtetl with its meadows and forests to the peasants of the surrounding villages who built houses on the land and established well-to-do manors in the style of wealthy villages. These were the so-called "hamlets"—small individual settlements that were scattered around the shtetl.

According to official sources, the year 1779 marked the beginning of a Jewish community. Until that time, it had been a small village, with a few peasant houses that the wealthy landowner built for his Podvisote serfs whose work was to chop down and uproot the old oaks. The wealthy landowner wanted to build a town near the Uman highway. For this purpose, he built a tavern in the forest and he settled a Jewish lessee there. This lessee was the first Jewish resident of Dubova.

In the last years there were more Jews than Christians in the shtetl. According to the census of the sugar commission at the Dubova cooperative, in 1918 there were 1,050 Christians and 2,500 Jews in Dubova.[2]

The shtetl Dubova lies eighteen versts from Uman. The highway into the city of Uman passes through wealthy villages and peasant settlements. Dubova at this time is also encircled by small forests of old oaks. Surrounding Dubova, spreading far and wide, is a wealthy settlement of flourishing Ukrainian villages, and between the fields and meadows of these villages are the well-established peasant manors of the newly rich hamlet peasants. Between village and shtetl flows the narrow Yatran River with its deep quiet waters that lead to the Bug River, and by its brightly washed banks, the peasant orchards and gardens bloom. On its high bank stands the old Dubova park with its shaded pathways, and downhill from there, planted with flowers and trees, is the Korzhova Palace that guards the area with patriarchal pride and old-monied comfort. Also standing at the river is the big mill which provided food for the Dubova Jews.

They were all involved in milling. Of the three hundred Jewish families in Dubova, one hundred and seventy traded in flour. The remainder were artisans and shopkeepers. On Thursday the neighboring peasants all brought their grain to market. The Dubova Jews bought it, ground it at the Dubova mill, and brought it to Uman or transported it to other cities. In this shtetl the Dubova Jews were very involved in developing the grain business in town. The mill there sated the surrounding peasant population with abundance, but they themselves barely eked out their small-Jewish-shtetl living. There were no rich people among them.

But in the last years of the war, during the Revolution, when flour was the most important product in the country, a treasure opened up for the Dubova Jews. For a bite of bread, the wealth of the city flowed in a stream of gold to the peasant population of the village. But this stream could not bypass Jewish hands, so a bit of the fortune that the Ukrainian peasants were gathering in casks and burying in the black earth did make it to the Jews.

But at some point, the wealthy village householders became jealous of the Jews who were flaunting their new wealth by throwing money around on expensive clothes and jewelry. Before this there had been no Christians involved in milling in Dubova. The exception was the priest who had a weakness for these Jewish businesses; he also used to mill in partnership with a Jew. But in the last years, when the Jews started being persecuted as speculators and having their merchandise taken away from them while transporting it, the peasants were simultaneously allowed to bring their products free and clear into town from their fields and homes. Thus the Dubova flour trade slipped out of Jewish hands and the Jews ended up living at the mercy of the peasants. Every time a peasant put his name on a Jewish wagon of flour heading for Uman, he took the greatest portion of the profits for himself and thought he was still doing the Jews a huge favor. So at the whim of a gang of happy young peasants, who were already in positions of power everywhere, they requisitioned the Jewish flour and distributed it among the poor peasant families in the village!

This is how the Jews in Dubova lived in the year 5679,[3] when the destruction of the Jewish communities in Ukraine began.

2

The political-cultural life of the Dubova Jews was rather underdeveloped. Raising of children was done in an old-fashioned manner. The children studied in the heder[4] from dawn to dusk. Afterward the talented children with keen minds went on to study with Dovid the shochet,[5] who was a replacement substituting for the old rabbi, and the few child prodigies were sent to the yeshiva to get rabbinic ordination or to become shochtim. Only the girls from the wealthy Dubova Jewish families studied at the zemstvo[6] school. The wealthy Christian children also studied there. In the summer students from outside Dubova came to give private lessons, but even though the shtetl was very close to Uman, the trend among Jewish youth to become nonmatriculated students, which was popular in all of the cities and shtetls, did not hold sway in Dubova.

Only the children of Gedalye Koretsky and the lawyer Nestrovsky completed their studies. During the Kerensky era[7] these two local intellectuals, along with the rabbi's son, Mendl Berditshevsky, founded a Jewish community school in the shtetl, where they themselves taught Hebrew, Yiddish, and Russian. They also invited the Dubova teacher, Pesach Zborsky, to teach Talmud, but the Dubova Jews were not interested in the Jewish school. Nobody even wanted to rent them a space, so they had to teach the children in the women's section of the synagogue.

Aside from these few intellectuals who were all Zionists, there was a Jewish pharmacist in Dubova who was ashamed of his Jewishness, similar to the Jews during the old Russian-Jewish Haskalah period.[8] He and his wife came from wealthy intellectual Uman families. They did not at all want to engage with the Jewish community of Dubova. They were only friends with Christians. Some of their regular visitors were Deviatkin, the zemstvo feldsher, who was afflicted with Jew-hatred, the midwife Shnuruk and her husband who was the administrator of the midwifery organization, both rabid Jew-detesters, and Police Superintendent Yanovich, the Black Militia[9] watchman of the old government and his wife. Only in Dubova would one perceive this as a natural occurrence. In short, he was a pharmacist who hated Jews and associated with antisemites.

Also there was Nestrovsky the lawyer, who publicly desecrated the Shabbos (the Sabbath), had a pig-treyf[10] kitchen in his Gentile-like house, and who naturally seldom gave even a copper groschen toward Jewish community activities and Jewish needs. Even his intellectual Zionist sons-in-law were unable to help with this.

And the rabbi of the shtetl was also from the old world. He, the elderly Reb Moyshe Arn Berditshevsky, who was blessed to have as a son Mikha Yoysef, was a simple man.[11]

His congregation chased after wealth and honor. The Dubova Jews were great merchants, from year to year the flour trade grew, and with the growth of the businesses the jealousy and hatred of one to the other and the lust for money also grew. They could never have enough golden ten-pieces, Nikolai money, Kerenskys, kronen, and pounds. Overall they couldn't sate themselves with the blessed green thousands. Even at the last minute before death the Dubova Jews could not part with them.

The Dubova Jews were great merchants, they knew what money signified, but the rabbi of the Dubova Jewish community was a modest man and would barely recognize a coin if he saw one.

The Dubova rabbi had a family, and when he was young he had small children that needed to be fed. In time the sons were old enough to be conscripted and the daughters to be married, but of all these matters having to do with money only the rebbetzin[12] had an inkling. The community parceled out yeast to her to sell, and thereby she managed from Shabbos to Shabbos.

Many years ago there was a good Gentile, a *Katsap*,[13] who leased out the mill. He couldn't bear to see the suffering of the rebbetzin who every Thursday went out with a sack borrowing a pood of flour, so he came up with the idea of forcing the Jewish flour merchants to give the righteous good rabbi a pound of flour from every sack, and from that time on it became an enforced duty. After this good Russian was gone, even though a few of the Jewish millers came and went, this tradition of giving a pound of flour to the rabbi remained forever. After the fire,[14] when they reconstructed the steam mill and the flour trade in Dubova grew, the rebbetzin became so rich with pounds of flour that she started baking challahs for Shabbos for all the widows and orphans of the shtetl.

But the rabbi was unaware of all of this. He was not interested in material matters. Day and night he only sat and studied, and if God sent him a good deed to do, he thanked Him for His grace and completed it in full.

That's how he healed his Jewish community from malaria many years ago. There was no doctor in the shtetl, and the Dubova Jews were then very poor, so their rabbi traveled to Uman and there collected a bit of money. With the money he bought quinine and a scale like those used in a pharmacy, and at home the entire family, the rebbetzin and the children, including the young Mikha Yoysef, got involved. Everyone made medicine. Afterward the rabbi himself went house to house every day and gave everyone the remedy, and this is how the shtetl was healed.

The rabbi did not interfere in community affairs. He detested conflicts, legal proceedings, and divorces. Overall he was very unhappy when he was torn away from studying. This is what he was like for the entire fifty years that he was the rabbi in Dubova.

Aside from the rabbi, the shtetl also took pride in the learned, pious, and righteous Pesach Zborsky, the Talmud teacher, who sat in his own small house and quietly studied Torah. There was also Omtsenyu,[15] a gem for God and humanity. He was Avrom Ukelman, the Dubova prodigy, who was raised as an only son by his mother, a young widow. She sent him to study in the great yeshivas of Lithuania, where at age seventeen he was ordained as a rabbi, destined to be a genius among Jews. Dubova also prided itself in the good and pious housewives who fed the Talmud Torah boys daily,[16] and also of Zlata, the butcher's wife with her blessed generous hand, who every evening would cook a meat dinner for respectable poor people to serve themselves and eat their fill.

3

Also in Dubova there were Jewish community leaders. The most respectable person in the shtetl was Gedalye Koretsky. He was also a Zionist (in Dubova there were no other parties aside from the Zionists). He came from a poor honest family. His father was a simple village Jew, but he had refined ideas about the upbringing of his children. Gedalye was a great Hebraist. As a young adult he received a diploma from the Russian gymnasium and became a university student, but for financial reasons he did not complete his studies.

For many years Gedalye Koretsky was the manager of Radokanaki's properties in Dubova.

Afterward he traded in grain and was a great merchant, but his way of life was very modest.

He provided his daughters with a higher education, sending them to study in the Russian capitals, and he never hired a maid in his home. His wife, Gishe Koretsky, was a simple woman, who in her later years became more cultivated, reflecting the examples of her husband and children. His ideal was physical labor. He alone kept his property in order, just as a good helper would, and Gishe, in front of the newly rich Dubova housewives who could not manage without maids, was also proud of her ability to care for her household alone.

In the last few years, the Koretsky family lived very frugally, because when the speculation began, he stopped trading and lived on limited groschen. Throughout this time he was totally engaged in work for the Jewish community. His house was always the center for all the Jewish community activities in Dubova, and he himself, the tall proud Jew with his prematurely gray hair, represented everywhere the Jewish community of the shtetl, where he was a crown and a jewel. During all three Russian dumas[17] he was the elector for the whole district of Uman. During the time of the Revolution he established a Jewish cooperative in Dubova, and he himself was its bookkeeper without pay. The Jews and Christians unanimously elected him to Kerensky's *volostnoe zemstvo*,[18] and during the time of the Bolsheviks they also elected him to the Ispolkom,[19] despite the fact that he had openly declared himself as a Zionist and as such he would remain. But he could not remain in the Ispolkom for very long. It was difficult for him to carry out the orders relating to Jewish speculators, who were being ambushed in the dark of night wherever they might be and caught with their wagons of merchandise. He witnessed how Jews were being ruined. In the course of one night, yesterday's well-to-do householders and up-and-coming rich became impoverished and reduced to begging at Gentile doors, and therefore he resigned from his position in the government, though throughout this time he worked in the Jewish cooperative that he had founded in the shtetl.

4

And Dubova had another Jewish community leader. This was Shmuel-Yitskhok Shkodnik, the Russian state tax collector. In his youth he was a horse trader and was poor. Afterward he became rich and owned forests, mills, and distilleries. Also for many years he was responsible for the kosher meat tax.[20] He was a vain person and a slick secular ignoramus with a good heart. He loved to be involved in community affairs, and he went after anyone who dared to assail his honor.

This particular Jew with his strong ambitions strived to be popular among the masses. He always argued with the rabbi and the learned of the shtetl and he unwaveringly took the side of the wagon drivers' minyan.[21] He was greatly valued in the surrounding peasant community. Because of his previous horse-trading at the fairs he was known by everyone. Also he loved to do a favor for a poor peasant, and quite often would lend a charitable amount without interest to buy a horse or a cow. He was also sympathetic to a poor Jewish person. But he himself wanted to be the head at the community table, and so he fought with each and every single person who stood up against him.

Shkodnik loved to live fancy. In Dubova he had a rich man's house, planted with trees and a valuable orchard alongside the home. He had no children, but one of the daughters of one of his wife's sisters was raised by him as his own child. The girl's mother was not a respectable person, she cast aside her husband and child and fell in love with a Gentile. Afterward she left with him for Uman, through all the years lived with him on the Gentile street, and in the end she herself converted. In Dubova they called her "Christia."

But her daughter grew up in the Shkodnik home and was a very good child. Her uncle married her off, choosing a cantor as her husband, and after this never took his eye off her either, just as if she were his own daughter. The niece's two older children were also raised in his house.

They were two beautiful and gifted young girls. As children they both completed the zemstvo school in Dubova. Their grandfather[22] hired for them at his home a Hebrew teacher and a second teacher for piano. Later he sent both of them to study in Uman. The older, Feyge-Vitele, went to business school, and the younger, Etele, studied at the gymnasium. Shkodnik and his wife did not have a chance to take as much delight in these two children as they wanted. They lived in Uman like daughters of the rich, and only during the summer would the girls stay with their grandfather in Dubova. It was very joyful then in Shkodnik's house. The two sisters were very beautiful. They both played piano and sang. The windows of the bright cozy rooms opened up onto the blossoming orchard, and the young people of the shtetl had a pleasant time in the beautiful and wealthy home of the tax collector.

But it was terrible that the two beautiful and wealthy girls did not like any Jewish young men. They both identified as Ukrainians, spoke Ukrainian, and mainly sought to spend time with young Ukrainians.

Here is how the gymnasium in Uman impacted the two beautiful Jewish girls from Dubova. Even at home the older sister, the tall and mature Feyge-Vitele, was truly always Ukrainian. Even as a child, studying in the zemstvo school, she loved to speak Ukrainian and sing Ukrainian songs. She loathed everything that was Jewish. But the gentle and wondrously beautiful Etele had been an ardent Jewish nationalist. She gladly studied Hebrew and always played and sang Yiddish folk songs.

They both became ardent Ukrainian nationalists in Uman. The two or three intellectual young men who often used to visit them in Uman would always find them with Ukrainian gymnasium students who were so insolent and rude to the Jewish guests of the two Jewish girls that they, the Jewish boys from Dubova, unanimously decided to stop visiting the two charming beautiful sisters in their home. Their only regular visitor was the peasant boy from Dubova, Markela Brishko.

5

Aside from the fine Zionist intellectual Gedalye Koretsky and, the honor-seeker in the community, Shmuel-Yitskhok Shkodnik, the narrow Dubova streets had their own active Jewish community worker. He was the wheelwright Moyshe Shvartsman.

He was born in Holovanivsk to a poor father, a storekeeper. Until he was ten years old he studied in the heder. From then until he was sixteen years old he went around jobless, and then he went away on his own to learn a trade. Afterward he got married in Khashchevate, and three years later settled in Dubova where some of his father's wealthy relatives lived.

He had a wheel workshop and worked very hard to sustain his wife and child, but he always had time for shtetl matters. Every community issue affected him personally, and he voiced his opinions at the community table at which the clever Dubova householders and learned people sat. But he always spoke to the point, and so people had to hear him out. In so doing he portrayed the toiling Jews of Dubova, using himself as an example. These particular people were rarely noticed in the old regime. They feared the impertinence and loudness of the toiling Jews, but Moyshe the wheelwright, who was outspoken and involved in everything, was nonetheless embraced by the Jewish community leaders. Even though he was from the boorish shoemaker street, he was a respectable person. He had refined thoughts, could speak with anyone, and understood each issue well, and as such the Dubova elite had given him a position on the former "town council."

During the old regime in Dubova this was the highest community position that Moyshe the wheelwright reached. But his true seven years of plenty began just after the Revolution. For the Jewish multitude of the shtetl, he was one of their own. He was also very much loved by the peasant population of the surrounding villages. This was not the same appreciation as that for Shmuel-Yitskhok Shkodnik, the former horse dealer who lived a rich man's life and did favors for poor Gentiles in the manner of an overly satiated rich man. For them Moyshe the wheelwright was their equal. For the entire surrounding area he made wheels for the peasants' wagons, and, standing at his workbench, he would chat pleasantly with every peasant, have a drink of vodka together, and wish each other well. Moreover, he was a poor man, always worried about how he would provide his seven small children with clothes and shoes. The only bourgeois luxury that Moyshe the wheelwright did not begrudge himself was that of giving an education to his beloved son Khananye.

Khananye was a very handsome and gifted boy. His father truly idolized him. Khananye was his oldest child, and all of Moyshe's great dreams from his own orphaned youth were bound up in Khananye. All the hopes that he was cheated out of during his entire life of toiling so hard in misery for a piece of bread became one goal and one great joy: to provide the opportunity for Khananye to develop his abilities.

Moyshe the wheelwright's son had the best melamdim and teachers. At age fourteen he knew Hebrew well. When it was time, his father prepared him for the entrance exams for the Uman Russian-Jewish gymnasium, where Khananye later became one of the best students, and in summer, when he would return to Dubova, his father was proud of him and felt lucky that the shtetl could claim his Khananye, one of the two Jewish gymnasium students, as their own.

Moyshe the wheelwright only wanted his son to become a doctor, and, though this was seen as a weakness, it was forgiven by Jews and Christians, and, after the Revolution, Moyshe was considered the number one and most important citizen in Dubova, elected to work in all the government institutions of the Peasants and Workers Republic.[23] At every meeting Gedalye Koretsky represented the wealthy Jewish residents of the shtetl, and he, Moyshe the wheelwright, the Jewish proletariat. There were also other Jewish representatives, but the responsibility for everything and everybody rested only with these two. The sensitive intellectual Gedalye could not manage his responsibilities for very long. At the first set of laws conflicting with Jewish interests his Jewish heart trembled, and he ran away. He hid in his neutral corner in the Jewish Cooperative, and Moyshe the wheelwright took his place. Moyshe did everything: he kept watch over the new order, quietly did favors for Jews, argued with his colleagues, the peasants who were already poisoned with Ukrainian Jew-hating nationalism, provided the newly-established Yiddish school with a space by requisitioning a house from a rich Jew from Dubova, and in this way he made Jewish enemies among the poor and rich of the shtetl.

But afterward everybody became good friends with him. When the entire Jewish community was saying viddui[24] in their cellars he was the only Jew in Dubova who knew how to talk to the bandits. It was his fate to survive the great destruction of the Dubova Jewish community and stand watch until the last breath of its last Jewish victim.

6

During the old regime there was no hatred between Jews and Christians in Dubova.

When the old priest was alive it was customary to carry the Christian dead through the shtetl, past the Jewish houses and shops, and no one was bothered by this. But when the young priest arrived in Dubova they began leading the Christian funeral processions through the peasant streets, bypassing the direct route, because the priest found it disgraceful to carry the crosses and holy images through the Jewish shtetl. But here is how the young priest dealt well with the Jews. He loved to trade. When the price of flour would rise he was unable to sit quietly in his home, but he didn't make a move without his Jewish partner. He was friendly with everyone involved in milling.

The peasants were also friendly in this way.

In the fifth year of the new priest when there were killings of Jews everywhere, suspicious-looking people came from Uman to Dubova and began to convince the Gentiles that the Jews of the shtetl wanted to slaughter all the Christians.

It was Friday evening. The peasants from the village streets took axes and pitchforks, went to the village leader to get him to ring the church bells for everyone to attack the Jews, because that night they wanted to kill off every last Christian. The peasant Adrian, who was then the village leader in Dubova, was an elderly man and by nature very tactical and calm. So he advised the agitated peasant crowd who were standing around him with axes and pitchforks to see what was happening in the shtetl first. To go see what the Jews were doing at that moment. If they were wanting to kill all the Christians that night, they most probably would be preparing themselves for it, so they should sneak up to the windows of the Jewish houses and see what was happening there.

The people were immediately convinced. They selected three priests from among themselves, and the village leader as the fourth. They would carefully go up to the windows and listen to what the Jews were doing in their houses at that moment.

It was a dark Friday evening in a small Jewish shtetl during the long nights of Kislev.[25] The mud was deep. The air was gnawing with humidity and cold. The Jews were exhausted from the week, and for the women it was a "short-Friday."[26] So the Dubova Jews ate their soup with noodles and lay down to sleep. Every Jewish window that the four representatives went to was dark, and the people were so deeply asleep that their snoring could be heard in the street. But one window was lit. This was at the rabbi's house.

A dark thought stole into the clever and calm village leader's mind. Everywhere they were already asleep, but at the rabbi's there was still light. Something must be happening there, perhaps they are getting ready there. Probably the oldest Jews of the shtetl had already gathered at the rabbi's, and they were making a plan for how to attack the Christians.

The four representatives stole up to the rabbi's house. Once again it was the same: quiet, everyone sleeping, the clock ticking, but on the cloth-covered sofa the rabbi was sitting alone in his gray housecoat with a yarmulke on the top of his head, bent over a book studying. The eight candlesticks that the rebbetzin had blessed were standing on the Shabbos table. The candles had already burned out. Only a small lamp lit the open book for the pale melancholic reader. From time to time he recited aloud, singing so sweetly, so poignantly ...

The village leader under the window could not contain himself. He burst out laughing and the other three representatives joined him. The rabbi was deeply immersed in his studies and did not even notice.

"So, a beheader ... ! Nothing to say!" Once again they laughed among themselves and went back to the volost to tell everyone how, despite their intent to kill everyone, the Jews were sleeping and their rabbi was sitting by himself at the table, dry as a stick, singing something out loud from a book. The Gentiles with their axes and pitchforks in their hands also laughed about the rabbi, the decapitator, singing something from a book. They simply enjoyed the story and completely fell over from laughter, and in this same good mood they all calmly dispersed to go home.

On the next day, Saturday morning, the Dubova Jews first found out the danger they had been in that night.

7

During the war years, the affable mood of the Ukrainian peasants changed, primarily from the time they began persecuting the Jewish speculators, and since the peasants were producers of the food products they gained exclusive control of the market. The peasants, after tasting easy earnings from trade, saw the Jews, with their experience and talent for commerce, as formidable rivals standing in their way everywhere.

After the Revolution the situation worsened. The oppressed Ukraine awakened with its desire for national liberation. The old Ukrainians were able to glimpse through the hazy veil of past centuries their memories of war, their romanticized love for freedom and the sword. Next came the intellectuals, who cloaked the Ukrainian romanticization of murder and blood in the brilliant lively colors of their national folk values.

And the terrain of the collapsing Russian state was favorable for battle. Two opponents stood one against the other: the village with its limitless natural sources of nourishment and the city with its feebly-developing technology and industry, and between city and village the Jewish middleman, seeking to earn his modest livelihood, thrashed about like a fish in water. He was a city person, a trustworthy attendant of the city inhabitants. The city was poor and didn't have any factories, the village did not want to provide grain to the city without pay, and in between there was the Jew. In the dark nights he wandered over hill and dale risking his own life, and brought forth to the city the best and most valuable of what the village produced.

In this way the conflict developed between the fed-up Ukrainian village bread providers and the hungry city proletarian *Moskal*.[27] Naturally, the Ukrainian intellectuals took the side of the Ukrainian peasantry and through symbols of freedom and national cultural evolution, glorified the simple economic interests of agrarian Ukraine. The Ukrainian intellectuals held the yellow-and-blue flag high and carried a portrait of Taras Shevchenko[28] like an icon through the villages. But the peaceful Ukrainian peasants, who year-in and year-out sowed and harvested their blessed black-earthed fields of grain, were Gonta's[29] grandchildren, and for three hundred years the Russian tsars held them in darkness, shackled in chains of servitude. Their unenlightened peasant minds understood their national economic interests in an unenlightened peasant way, just as their grandparents once did in the years 5408 and 5409.[30]

And at the same time the Ukrainian intelligentsia was fully responsible. It was they, the intellectuals, who added fuel to the fire. They, in their quarrel with the city Muscovite who had seized power in the country, could not find a better approach for engaging with the unenlightened peasantry than to incite the countryside against the innocent Jewish population of the cities and shtetls, exterminating all of them with helpers from among the Muscovites.

Afterward the intelligentsia had great remorse over this. Even for the intellectual nerves of Khmelnytsky's heirs,[31] the slaughtering of the Jews was too gruesome. But it was already too late. They did not have the power to halt the rivers of

Jewish blood that they themselves had called for. But it was actually the Muscovites who halted it with their iron might of fire and sword, and the Ukrainian intellectuals were branded in history as bandits and murderers.

8

The intelligentsia in Dubova were few in number. Most of them were freshly-baked intellectuals from rich peasant families who became cultured. The hero of the Ukrainian national movement in Dubova was Markela Brishko, the especially close friend of Shkodnik's grandchildren.

He was the son of a wealthy peasant. His father had a beautiful house in Dubova with rich orchards. Markela completed the zemstvo school where many Jewish students studied, and among them were also the two sisters Feyge-Vitele and Etele. After completing the local school, for a while he was a teacher in Dubova and gave lessons in Jewish homes. Afterward he became a writer for the volost. He remained in this position until he was mobilized to the military. At the front the Austrians captured him and sent him to Galicia. He came out of prison ill and they let him go home to recover. Overall, he was sickly, thin, scrawny, and always so pale as if he had just gotten better from an illness.

Markela Brishko did not return to the military. After the Revolution he went to Uman and attended Ukrainian teacher-training courses there. At that time he became a frequent guest of the Shkodnik's grandchildren. When they were home he would often visit them at their grandfather's. For the first Bolsheviks Markela was a secretary in the Dubova militia administration and in secret worked for the Ukrainian movement. He also used to organize Ukrainian-language theatre performances.

The second intellectual who at that time worked along with Brishko in the secret Ukrainian committees was his relative Andrei Ovtsharuk, who also used to frequent Shkodnik's house. He too was a peasant youth from Dubova, but he completed the four-grade school in the village of Babanka and afterward the military school in Kyiv. He came to Dubova already an officer.

When Petliura[32] came to power, Ovtsharuk joined the military and adopted Petliura's Ukrainian approach: he and Brishko used to drive around the villages and agitate the peasants against the communists and Jews who all wanted to dominate the Ukrainian people. In Dubova secret meetings were also organized for this purpose. Every Sunday Ukrainian intellectuals of the shtetl and of the surrounding villages would gather at the home of Shnuruk the midwife, who also identified with the Ukrainians, and they would develop all sorts of plans there.

They were all there at that meeting. Present were the priest's son, a student at the Kyiv Polytechnic, and his second son, a seminarian. The former steward of the Podvisote estates, who was reputed to be an earnest person and a good family man, was very punctual. With him also came Demsky, a polite and quiet manager for the noble property owners of Korzhova, followed by the two young Poles who worked with him in his office. But the most energetic of them all was Deviatkin, the young feldsher, with his cynically brutal jokes about the impending Jewish massacres. Listening very earnestly to Deviatkin was Grabovetski, the owner of the Dubova mill, who was an officer with Petliura, and watching him with a chuckle was the elderly and good-natured veterinarian Longvinov. Also among the important attendees was the former postman Melnik, who while in Petliura's army became the postmaster and from then on he openly and freely agitated to exterminate the Jews because they were all communists. They also brought the other postman, Kartshinski, into the secret intellectual circle of Dubova. He was also promoted by the Petliura authority to a high post in the zemstvo administration.

Also Moniuno, the former sailor who was a committed Ukrainian nationalist, used to come with Kartshinski to the meetings. Prior to Kerensky and the Bolsheviks, the peasants voted Moniuno into all the institutions. Shnuruk, the midwife, used to invite all of them as guests to her Sunday table, where they were accustomed to not even getting a little taste of vodka. The meetings were conducted over a sober glass of tea. The people were very earnest, they were thinking about a huge Jewish massacre, and the zealous leaders were unquestionably Brishko and Ovtsharuk.

After the pogroms in Proskuriv[33] and in Teplyk,[34] the Jews in Dubova began to fear the two local peasant intellectuals, Markela and Andrei—and Khaye Shkodnik, Shmuel-Yitskhok's wife, found it necessary to calm the people, saying Markela and Andrei visited the children because they, Feyge-Vitele and Etele, spoke Ukrainian very well. They said that when they spoke to someone in their own language it made them feel good.

Brishko and Ovtsharuk used to happily spend the evening at Shkodnik's house, playing and singing Ukrainian folk songs, while during the day they rode through the villages with clandestine calls to prepare for a Jewish slaughter. And so the Dubova Jewish youth avoided Shkodnik's house as if it were a nest of evil. Even the pharmacist Moyshe Tshernov, who loved to speak Ukrainian, who was close with Markela and Andrei because they were classmates in the zemstvo school, and who also was madly in love with Feyge-Vitele, began to shun Shkodnik's house and his grandchildren, the Ukrainians.

9

It happened. The seeds that the Ukrainian intelligentsia sowed in the Ukrainian earth bloomed far better than they had anticipated. On Sunday May 11, 1919, the peasant conference in Uman opened. It was shut down on the same day. The peasant representatives of the 105 volosts, who comprised the majority of the conference, opposed the authority of the city-proletarian minority. The authority had demanded that only communists be elected to the Presidium, and the Ukrainian nationalist peasant majority did not want to concede to this.

The Uman Ispolkom shut down the conference, declared a state of siege, and ordered the agitated peasant delegates to go home. At the same time the Ispolkom arrested Shtogrin,[35] the former student of the Uman horticultural school, who was an important leader in the Ukrainian national movement and who during the conference openly agitated against the power of communists and Jews, calling the peasants to arms.

This was on Sunday afternoon, and on that evening Gol, the Jewish commissar, informed the rabbi in Uman that the authority was deserting the city. But on the next day, Monday morning, Gol begged the rabbi not to tell anyone, because what he told him was based on a misunderstanding, and at that very moment they heard shooting from all directions. The communists had to leave the city at once. At 11 in the morning the peasant partisans,[36] under the leadership of the Ukrainian leftist "S-R"[37] Klimenko, entered Uman. Immediately joining them were the wealthier Christians from the environs of Uman, the escaped arrestees, and a portion of the Christian student youth.

It was the 12th of May. The delegation of the Jewish community who wanted to meet with Klimenko had to remain where they were, because the Jewish dead were already lying in the streets.

On the 13th of May the enthusiastic leaders of the Ukrainian peasants let the partisans know that the Jewish authority had already fallen, and they should not listen to any zhid[38] agitators. At the same time the bells of all the Uman churches were ringing, and the Black priest Nikolski[39] led a Christian procession through the streets with holy songs of praise. On the same day they forced three Uman Jews to dig graves for themselves.

Meanwhile Shtogrin fled to his large village Stari Babany, and there he incited the peasants to fight. Under his leadership the remaining delegates of the shut-down conference did the same in other villages and shtetls. And in this way Dubova too caught fire.

10

Of the two representatives that Dubova had sent to the Uman conference, one of them disappeared somewhere. It was Zarotshinski, the former Black Sea sailor. He was a committed and dedicated socialist, and as such naturally he immediately saw that the Ukrainian national movement was becoming a shameful bloodletting of the Jewish population. On the same day the second delegate returned to Dubova and reported that the communists had disbanded the conference. Immediately Brishko left Dubova on foot for Uman.

Brishko returned home on the 12th of May. He went directly to the Ispolkom and presented a mandate from Klimenko that he, Brishko, was appointed the commander of Dubova. Then he began to speak about Jews and communists. They, the Jews, wanted to seize power in Ukraine. If one needed a teacher in the local school, one first had to ask whether he knew Yiddish. And immediately Brishko ordered all the members of the Ispolkom, Jews and Christians, to meet together. Because he had an order to remove the Jews from authority, he then told the five Jewish members to leave and the Christians to remain. At that instant the former Baltic fleet sailor Kopnik asked him, "How can we be sure that this is the truth?" To this Brishko answered that they should send someone to see what was happening in the city, and the Ispolkom did so. They immediately sent two trustworthy people to Uman, who returned in the evening and brought arms from the Ukrainian peasant authority.

The Christian members of the Dubova Ispolkom immediately recognized the new authority and united themselves with Brishko. Aside from Zarotshinski, the deserter from the Red Fleet, they were all local people: Grabovetski, the owner of the Dubova mill, a student of Petliura, who held a position in the Ukrainian national movement equal with that of the sailor Moniuno; Vasili Smelnitski, the hog dealer, who was even a "free thinker" because he wandered for years through Finland and the Petrograd area, from which he returned in city clothes, bringing a lot of money and a refined city woman as a wife. They also said about him that he had in his possession the picture of Lenin and Trotsky, and that he once told someone that they were great men. Nonetheless he recognized the Jewish danger toward the Ukrainian peasants, and, standing by his hogs in the market and speaking with the people, he never minced words about Jews and Judaism.

And Kopnik, strutting in his old worn-out sailor cap from the flame-red Baltic fleet, was an easygoing person overall. It was all the same to him. He could recognize each and every authority separately, as long as every day he had something to smoke and a good drink of hard liquor. Sokolov, the former justice of the peace, was an equally cool townsman too. For him, an elderly man-of-the-world with a fine taste for ladies, whichever principles the authority would establish in the country were all the same. Now in his older years, just as in his youth, he still loved life and women. The remaining two or three members of the Ispolkom were simple village folk who did everything they were ordered to do. The fifteen Dubova militiamen also immediately adapted themselves to the new order.

Monday evening, on the 12th of May, there was a top-secret meeting at the midwife Shnuruk's house. The work was immediately divided up among the intellectuals. Everyone was enthusiastic and patriotically inclined. They committed themselves to accomplishing the "holy" task until its end.

After this meeting Brishko distributed weapons to the local militia, and on Tuesday the 13th of May he rode around the neighboring villages all day. The Jews of the shtetl looked at him in fear and wanted to know what was going on. Moyshe the wheelwright and two other Jewish young men who were friendly with him on a first-name basis, threw themselves at him with pleas for him to privately tell them the truth, whether there was any danger threatening the Jewish population of the shtetl. To this Markela curtly answered them, "Something has to happen here, and I guarantee that there will be sacrifices ..."

This particular answer stirred up the shtetl with fright, and Gedalye Koretsky himself turned to the old Jewish ways. He found a good moment to talk it through with Brishko as one would do with a smart person from town. He invited him to his house to drink a glass of coffee on Tuesday evening. There he told him the truth, politely and gently, that he, Gedalye Koretsky, as a Jew loyal to his people who bled for the fate of all Jews, was delighted that the communists were giving up their authority, because communism was ruining the Jewish population who made their living from trade, and he hoped that the Ukrainian peasantry would act with greater fairness towards the Jewish citizens of the land. But now in this difficult moment, when the authority was changing, one could find bad elements everywhere that wanted to make trouble. Therefore, in the name of the Dubova Jews he was begging Brishko to guard the shtetl, and for this he would be given a contribution of 100,000 Nikolai rubles. After all, maintaining a guard would cost money.

Brishko listened to him attentively until the end, but he refused to take the money and once again answered him very curtly and ambiguously, "If I deserve it, then you will give me money."

After this second answer the turmoil in the shtetl became even greater. People were afraid to spend the night at home. Young and old fled in terror and fear into the back alleys looking for protection in the small hunched-over houses of artisans and poor people.

11

It was Tuesday, Pesach Sheni,[40] 5679.

At nightfall in the shtetl there were a few machine-gun volleys, designated signals to attack the Jews, and the peasants of Dubova's surrounding villages tore into the shtetl with axes and pitchforks.

All of them were local Gentiles. They were all wearing their coats inside-out and the visors of their hats turned backwards. The inside-out coats and turned-around visors were symbols of the overturned order in the country. Many of them painted their faces so that they would not be recognized. But the Dubova Jews recognized everybody. From the feldsher, to the former mailman Kartshinski, to the most insignificant peasant child who ran after them like an enraged dog, they were all recognizable to the Jews. They killed all their victims with cold steel, and for amusement they fired gunshots into the desolate streets. That night thirteen people perished by all sorts of violent deaths. It was mainly the Jewish families that had conflicts with the local peasants who suffered. The family of Dovid Furman the butcher also suffered in this way.

Moreover, he lived on a back street. Therefore, all his relatives and good friends came to him to hide. They also were all certain that, because he was very friendly with the Gentiles, they would not do anything bad to Dovid the butcher. From one market day to the next they entrusted their cattle to him without payment, and he would parcel out meat to them, letting them pay for it when they had money. Besides, with her generous hand his wife was known for helping people in need. It was specifically Zlata, the butcher's wife, who every night cooked a meat soup for the respectable poor people of the shtetl. Standing near the meat, this Jewish woman knew of the poor Gentiles whose husbands did not return home from the war and the disabled male and female beggars who used to sit near the church with outstretched hands for a donation of a groschen. She kept everyone alive with some chicken giblets. On the Dubova market days she was always surrounded by all kinds of Gentile women who asked favors of her, and said of her that God gave her a good Christian soul.

And on the night of Pesach Sheni the greatest misfortune actually happened to this Zlata.

This mishap was an accident. They were searching her house for another Jew, also a butcher, with whom a Dubova peasant neighbor of his had a dispute over a piece of land. So on the night when killing Jews was allowed, that man asked his pals to get even with his Jewish neighbor for him.

This Moyshe the butcher whom they were looking for was not actually hiding at Furman's, but it was long after midnight, the blood of the attackers was already boiling over, so wielding rifles, axes, and pitchforks, they, along with Kartshinski the former mailman, stormed into Dovid Furman's house, which was full of frightened Jewish men, women, and children. The attackers immediately blew out the lamp so they wouldn't be recognized, and against the moonlit windows amidst yells and screams they began hacking right and left. A few of the attackers feverishly began robbing the closets and the dresser drawers. Within a couple of minutes, they had killed Zlata's sister and her husband whose seven children that night were able to tear out of the house and escape into the peasant gardens. Also, two children of Zlata's brother Arn-Zekharye Kozodoy, eight and ten years old, and two neighbors, a young woman and an elderly mother, were killed. At the same time Zlata herself barely made it through the night alive. She threw herself between the raised axes and pitchforks, pleading with the local bandits, calling them by their names. She kissed their hands and begged for mercy to stop them from killing. They axed at her head, cut off one of her hands, and gouged an eye out of her four-year-old daughter whom she was holding in her arms.

In the end they had mercy on her. When she fell, fainting along with her child, one of the murderers cried out, "Brother, it is Zlata! Look at what you are doing to poor Zlata!"

With this cry they lowered their hands with the axes and it became dead-silent. This is how it was for a few moments. Suddenly someone uttered in fear, "Is Moshke not here? Then where is he?"

The leaden voice of Dovid Furman cried out from a corner, "Call a doctor …"

Once again one of the bandits with the inside-out coat and turned-around cap uttered with regret, "Poor Zlata!," but at that moment somebody shot through the moonlit window, and with the clanging of the shattered glass they all ran away from the house.

12

On the 14th of May, on Wednesday morning, not one Dubova Jew was seen in the street. The dead were lying in the houses, and the living were sitting with them petrified by fear. In the afternoon a few gathered strength and went out to take a look at what was happening in the vicinity. Here and there somewhere by a fence one could stumble upon a murder victim. The street that was resounding with wailing women again became silent. People with waxen faces appeared, carrying the wounded past the houses to the hospital. They were also carrying the pregnant hacked Zlata Furman on a makeshift gurney. She kept fainting. In the early morning a Gentile neighbor brought Zlata's wounded son to the hospital. Weeping Gentile women also brought her the young girl with the gouged-out eye.

In the evening forty peasants from the Korzhova area, armed with guns and swords, came into Dubova with harmonicas and song. They stopped in the market to sharpen their sabers, and a shrill grating sound of sharpened metal arms was heard. The Jews immediately started to run into the fields and the surrounding peasant gardens, and the newly arrived peasants ran after them firing their guns.

Most of those who ran away were killed in the fields. The savagery of the attackers was even more gruesome this time. They cut off tongues, noses, and ears, chopping limbs right off of living people. The two peasants Kirilo Tsherniuk and Martin Zborzhevski were the most savage of all.

Both were residents of Dubova, with land, decent homes, wives, and children. Kirilo's daughters were welcomed as servants into the Jewish homes, but they were both outcasts in the Dubova peasant community. Martin had been sentenced to hard labor for robbery and murder. He came home at the time of the Revolution. Kirilo had also been arrested for robbery many times. But in this historical moment they were both in Dubova and became heroes of the Ukrainian national movement.

Thursday during the day someone posted an order from Klimenko on the street not to rob or kill any peaceful residents; by doing so one disgraced the Ukrainian authorities.

Immediately Brishko positioned the militia at the bridge, not allowing peasants to ride into the market which was held every Thursday in Dubova. All the bandits rushed back to their homes in the surrounding villages, but Kirilo and Martin still did not want to put down their axes.

During this period he, Kirilo, felt happy as a clam. On Thursday morning he sent a young boy to Moyshe the wheelwright with a note saying that they should raise 10,000 rubles for him. To this Moyshe answered Kirilo that he had to wait until evening. The Jewish community leaders immediately held a meeting in Gedalye Koretsky's house, and it was decided that they must meet with Brishko and beg him to disarm Kirilo. In the meantime, they raised the 10,000 rubles, but they gave it to Brishko for him to divide it among his young gang. Brishko promised to guard the shtetl and that he would shoot bandits on the spot …

But in the meantime, Kirilo took action. After Moyshe the wheelwright didn't give him any money, he killed the girl Sonye Shoshkin in the garden of one of his neighbors. Her father had died, and along with her elderly mother she owned a small store on the Gentile street. She had hidden herself in the peasant gardens where she encountered Kirilo who shot her in the head. Wounded, she ran into the river, but he dragged her out and back to the garden and hacked off a few of her limbs, proclaiming at each hack, "That's for your sugar, that's for your salt, that's for your matches!" …

Already at that time Klimenko's order had been posted near the volost. Jews came out into the streets to gather the dead who were strewn in the fields and gardens. This is how someone found Sonye's scattered bones around which the dogs from the neighboring yards were already circling. They gathered them up into a sack and put them on the wagon to bring to the cemetery, where there already lay another sack with the bones of the grain broker Yisroel-Leyb Gutes, whom they had killed in the field. A Jewish woman from a village had gathered his hacked-off limbs at the risk of her own life.

Not a single Gentile was to be seen in the street. Upon seeing the mutilated Jewish dead on the wagons, all the Gentile women took down their stands and left the market, and the peasant children fled from the street in terror. The women's choked wailings still resounded in the dead silence. Immediately there was a frightening turmoil: Jews abandoned the dead and ran to wherever their eyes took them. Kirilo ran through the street with his bloodied ax and ran like that into Gedalye Koretsky's house. Kirilo demanded 10,000 rubles from Koretsky and threatened him with the ax. But at that moment Brishko himself came to Koretsky's house and commanded Kirilo to give him the ax. But Kirilo mocked Brishko, saying, "Don't you know that we must now kill Jews," and angrily yelled at him, "It was the Zhids who bought you off, so you gave an order not to kill!"

Hearing these last words Brishko grabbed his gun and on the spot he shot Kirilo dead with two bullets.

Brishko then ordered the militia to lay Kirilo's dead body in the market for people to look at, and he dispatched four members of his gang from the village to make an end of Martin too. The four young peasant men captured Martin in a forest not far from Dubova. There they shot him on the spot, and even brought his dead body to the center of the market so that young and old would see what the Ukrainian authorities would do to bandits.

13

It was Thursday the 15th of May. In Uman Klimenko had already issued the second proclamation: they had to stop the bloodshed because the zhid authority[41] had already been overthrown and there were also many innocents among them.

It occurred on the fifth day of the Uman massacre. Upon seeing the mountains of Jewish corpses strewn in the streets, the heroic leaders of the Ukrainian national movement were frightened by their success. Also frightened were the misled and incited Christian masses from the outskirts of Uman. For five days in a row the rampaging bandits of the previous night had been deafened by the church bells, and now, drunk with Jewish blood and spoils, they looked superstitiously at those killed and tortured by their own hands. They themselves rushed to the Jewish cemetery, seeking a place to get the dead out of sight as quickly as possible. And on the fifth day, when the Jews came out of their cellars and started running to the cemetery to dig individual graves for their nearest and dearest whom the Gentiles had in fear thrown together into two mass graves, an angered gang of local Gentiles, fearing that the Jews might later take revenge, blocked their way and ordered the Jews not to touch the dead.

But on the same day numerous armed peasants from the villages came into the city, sent to take revenge on the Jews because the Jews were poisoning the wells and the blessed Garden of Eden waters of Uman to kill all the Christians. This particular false accusation regarding poisoning the water was also widespread among the Christian inhabitants of the city, and so Klimenko for a second time had to come out against the bloodshed. But this time his armed peasants accused Klimenko of being bought by the Jews, just as the Dubova bandit Kirilo had accused Brishko.

Then Nomak, another leader of the Ukrainian national movement, came forth. He clearly declared that the bloodshed brought great disgrace on the liberated Ukraine, because the people's rule was being shamed by the European nations. At the same time a Christian voice of compassion was heard as well. The religious teachers of the Uman schools proclaimed that one should have love for everyone, as Christ himself commanded. ...

This happened on the 15th of May, and three days later the Ukrainian intellectuals found it necessary a third time to explain to the people that they did not intend any massacres but only to establish the Ukrainian people's authority. The resolutions that were adopted at the second peasant conference in Uman were intended for the "soviets" to implement only against the Russian bastard and zhid leadership and the commissars that crucified Christ.

Meanwhile they advised the Jewish community of Uman to send a delegation to present a welcoming address to the conference, and on the same day the opposition committee[42] released a call for peace with all inhabitants of the Ukrainian lands, explaining that Jews also suffered at the hands of the communists. And as a rule, we don't take actions against ethnic groups, but only against those that take everything and give nothing.

The conference still considered it its duty to absolve the Ukrainian peasantry of the Uman massacre, casting the blame fully on the Christian populace of the city, whom they therefore did not let into the meeting hall. They also reproached the city intellectuals for their terrible agitation against innocent people.

But these honorable ways of helping came too late. The city's Christian middle class and the peasants were already poisoned with the bandits' venom against the Jewish population, which ended up forsaken. In Uman, in broad daylight, Gentile women went out with sacks, dragging everything from the unguarded Jewish houses and stores, whatever their hands could grab, and the Christian children played in the streets with the dead bodies. Schoolboys would shoot at them for target practice. Others searched the dead, shaking out their pockets, looking for watches, cigarette cases, and money.

In the villages and the shtetls, the civil war flared up in a wildly strange manner. The Soviet punitive brigade rooted out those who revolted against the Moscow government with fire and sword, and the Ukrainian peasantry responded with killings and slaughtering of the Jews in accordance with the old methods of Gonta and Khmelnytsky. All that was left for the Ukrainian intellectuals to do was to call for order on paper and to obey the laws of the Ukrainian authorities on paper.

14

During these days Markela Brishko, the Ukrainian intellectual of Dubova, obeyed the laws of the newly-independent Ukraine. He organized a voluntary battalion of Dubova and village peasant youth, and they guarded the shtetl from robbery and murder. On Thursday night the Jews were afraid to sleep in their homes and were standing on guard, with their bundles aloft, ready to flee at any moment. But it was quiet.

On Friday they once again started bringing the corpses from the fields and peasant gardens. In the cemetery women were lamenting, resounding the air with their wails, and in the evening there was a frightening commotion in the shtetl. They found out that Markela Brishko had taken Feyge-Vitele, Shkodnik's granddaughter, to be converted.

This conversion was a definite thing, so it was clear that during the great days of the Ukrainian liberation Brishko had his own romantic interests in mind as well.

On Tuesday evening, when the massacre had just begun, many people ran to Shkodnik's house to hide. Shkodnik took in everyone who came to him. But he himself did not feel good about this and was very upset. He responded to everyone, "I will remain in the attic of my house by myself, no matter what God brings."

Shkodnik's house was, as expected, bypassed, and those who hid there during the night survived. But on the second night Shkodnik's house was not so safe, because his two grandchildren, Feyge-Vitele and Etele, said that they couldn't hide so many people with them. They were also scared for themselves, and so Shkodnik recommended that everyone sit in their own houses and wait for whatever God would bring.

Late at night both girls told their grandfather and grandmother that they were really afraid to sleep at home. Markela Brishko sent a soldier for them so that they could sleep at his father's in the village. He advised their grandfather and grandmother to go there too. Their house would be safe, no one was going to touch it.

Shmuel-Yitskhok Shkodnik immediately replied that he would stay at home and she, Khaye Shkodnik, also agreed not to leave the house, but Feyge-Vitele and Etele got dressed to leave. An armed soldier was waiting in the yard. They kissed their grandfather and grandmother and left.

But Feyge-Vitele never returned to her grandfather's house. In the morning Etele came home in the company of the same armed soldier, and she told her grandparents that Fanye[43] was going to stay where she was. She was betrothed to Markela. They would both be traveling that day to Korzhova to the priest where they would get married.

The vain Shmuel-Yitskhok calmly and in silent anger listened to this, as if one of his enemies from the shtetl community were standing before him. As always, his wide brow was smooth and clear. He stroked his beard and left for his study, and there he isolated himself for an entire twenty-four hours and would not allow anybody in. Thus she, Khaye Shkodnik, wrung her hands in woe and burst into such a high-pitched wail along with Feyge-Vitele's mother (who had just arrived at the time of the misfortune) that Etele fled the house in fear to her good Christian friends, the former police superintendent Yanovich and his wife, and had not been home for several days in a row.

After this, on early Friday evening, when it was quiet in the shtetl and Brishko had given permission for the dead to be taken to the cemetery, Khaye Shkodnik ran out into the street wailing and clamoring that Markela had made off with Feyge-Vitele from the house the night before and took her to Korzhova to the priest. At night Markela had come with two soldiers, opened a window next to the garden, and carried Feyge-Vitele out through the window. Etele heard all of this, but she was too afraid to respond. On the next street Feyge-Vitele's mother, Reytse the cantor's wife, wailed and grieved in the same manner.

And a fear fell upon all the mothers of Dubova who had grown daughters. He, Markela, was coming at night with soldiers to drag Jewish girls to be converted ....

It was Friday evening. The dead were still lying in the streets, and in the houses the blood had not yet been washed away from all the walls and doors, and the darkness of Friday night was approaching with a rainstorm. But in the shtetl it was noisy as if in a market. Jewish men and women were running about as if they were drugged, looking for wagons. Before candle lighting on Friday, during a rainstorm, all the Dubova girls were sent to Holovanivsk, placed under the custody of their local Jewish self-defense organization.

15

The voluntary military division, which Brishko organized with the local peasant youth to guard the shtetl, happened to be in the nearby village of Korzhova. In accordance with the request of Moyshe the wheelwright, they, along with the ataman[44] and the Dubova militia, came to the cemetery to survey the corpses of those who had been killed with such violence and the sacks of bones that had been gathered in the fields. It was Saturday, after prayers. Based on the order of the rabbi, Jews left the synagogues and began to bury the dead, because the heat was so strong that delaying this until the next day was a danger for the living. This took place very quietly. Brishko told them not to cry, because the wailing of the women would frighten the peaceful residents in the surrounding village streets.

It was a quiet Shabbos in Dubova. They quietly came home from the cemetery and quietly sat shiva.[45] But they didn't complete sitting shiva, because during that night the volunteer soldiers of Brishko's military division began wandering around the shtetl and attacking Jewish houses. Afterward they became bolder and did the same by day. They would beat every single Jew that came into their sight in the back streets. A few days passed like this. The "quiet" Jewish community, whom they had ordered not to cry, became restless, and the proletarian member of the Jewish community council, Moyshe the wheelwright, began to look for ways to deal with this.

Once Moyshe spoke in a comradely manner with a group of these armed peasant youth and unbeknownst to the ataman secretly asked them how to get on their good side so that they would guard the shtetl properly.

They listened to him and answered honestly that they wanted money.

Moyshe summoned the most respectable householders to Gedalye Koretsky's house, and he proposed that they establish a monetary fund that would always be available during terrible times to ransom the shtetl from robbery and death. If not, he would refuse to do anything, and would see to leaving with his family for somewhere else where their lives were not in such danger. The people became very uneasy at these words, and Gedalye Koretsky tried to explain to him what being homeless would mean for a household with seven small children. "It would be a great misfortune for this shtetl if you left. If they saw you do this, everybody would flee, and their meager possessions would remain for anyone to take." Moyshe the wheelwright let himself be persuaded. They promised him they would establish a monetary fund, and he himself undertook the task of coming to an agreement with Brishko to take money to guard the shtetl.

Meanwhile in Uman the situation of the Ukrainian nationalists worsened. On the 21st of May the peasants with the inside-out coats and the turned-around hats left the city and returned to the villages, taking their weapons and the stolen Jewish goods with them. After the Jewish slaughter in Uman they believed that their mission was over. They did not want to go to the front to fight against the organized troops of the Soviet authority. In general, it felt odd to them to go far from their local Uman area, and it was their work season. There was work to be done in the fields. They would soon have to cut and rake the hay in the meadows.

On the night of May 22nd, once they had fortified themselves for several days, the Red Army went into Uman after a battle on the outskirts of the city. Also that night news came that the Soviet punitive brigades of the villages had shot

Shtogrin, the inspired hero of the Ukrainian movement, who had a great influence on the peasantry. Klimenko along with fifty horsemen fled the city to recruit new soldiers from the peasant communities to battle with fresh strength against the Soviet troops.

And so late at night Klimenko passed by Dubova, and three of his horsemen went into the shtetl with a hoorah and whistling ... Jewish men woke up in bed scared to death, women fell into a faint, and at the same time someone risked his life and went out in the bright moonlight to Moyshe the wheelwright for him to do something.

Moyshe got dressed to go out in the street to seek militiamen or any of Brishko's gang members. Standing around him were his seven children, who were bewailing him as if he were dead. His wife heroically blocked his way with both hands. She would not let him go. "Aren't there any other leaders in town? Everybody is hiding, and when it comes to trouble it is only you."

The pained and exhausted Moyshe the wheelwright calmed his wife and children, "I will come back soon." He lit a cigar and went into the street.

But nothing bad happened. Moyshe ran through the back gardens to the militia administration, and he took a militiaman and went with him around the shtetl to see who was making a commotion and whistling. This is how they ran into Klimenko's three horsemen in the street. They greeted them in a friendly manner, and Moyshe asked if they needed anything. By the light of the moon they showed Moyshe that they were wearing torn boots. They also complained that they were hungry and parched from heat and dust.

"What is this?" Moyshe answered them with a smile. "There are actually decent people living here .... Are we already, God help us, such that we would not take in and offer food to a Ukrainian soldier? Come to me, brothers!"

Moyshe and the militiaman went first, and the three horsemen followed.

When Moyshe arrived at the house he went in to calm the children and ordered his wife to prepare the table, to set out vodka, and to give them the best food that she had to eat in the house. The soldiers tied up their horses and went into the Jewish home to rest. They immediately sat down at the table, drank up and snacked amicably, and this is how they spent the entire evening. Meanwhile they told Moyshe that the Red "heathens" went into Uman and that Ataman Klimenko went once again out to the villages to recruit men.

It was already midday when they warmly said goodbye to the hospitable Dubova Jew, and when Moyshe led them out of the yard he gave them 3,000 Kerensky rubles for boots.

16

Two days later Klimenko rode in a carriage to Dubova, encircled by his fifty horsemen, and he left behind in the village of Babanka, a few versts from the shtetl, the partisans that he had assembled from the nearby villages. He visited one of his uncles, the peasant Stafia Kazak, who became a wealthy and well-established landowner of fields and gardens in Durilin's territory, near the old Dubova settlement. Klimenko's horsemen remained in the shtetl and began cavorting in the market near the Jewish food shops. Immediately the Jews closed their stores and ran away, looking for a proper channel to Ataman Klimenko. In this instance the best intermediary for the Jews was Klimenko's uncle Stafia Kazak. Stafia was a decent neighbor to two Jews from Uman who had an oil factory near his property. During the nights of the killings Stafia and his wife and child hid them in his granary, and so the two Jewish factory owners pleaded with the amiable Kazak for him to put in a good word to Ataman Klimenko on behalf of the Dubova Jews. He, the ataman, should order the local partisan group to guard the shtetl from bad people.

The rich peasant honestly fulfilled their request, and he gave a brief moral lecture to his sister's son, that he was too easygoing with his young partisan group and that there was nobody in charge of his property. And one should also have compassion for all human beings even if they were not Christians ... Klimenko heartily clapped Stafia on his back for standing up for the Jews. This actually pleased Klimenko. He said that he would immediately call together a meeting in the volost and that the Jews of the town should send a delegation there.

Naturally, the usual representatives, Moyshe the wheelwright and Gedalye Koretsky, went. They took along another important householder, because he was a tall handsome man with a round black beard, as an embellishment.

Gedalye Koretsky stood up to speak before Klimenko and the large peasant group that he assembled. But he was very upset, tears stuck in his throat. So he called upon Moyshe to tell the peasant authorities about the great suffering of the Jews, and he, Moyshe, told them in his simple manner that he was a worker, that with his own ten fingers he fed himself and his wife and children, and like everyone there, he held dear his possessions that were earned with his own sweat. And he asked the peasants at the meeting to point out to him which Jew in Dubova was a communist. "Everyone together, Jews and Christians, will tear that person to pieces."

Voices from the peasant people were heard, "Should we give you a paper that you are allowed to live on our Ukrainian land? And what about your people tormenting our peasants in Holovanivsk?"

Klimenko himself responded to these words. He told them that they were mixing together the bad elements with the innocents. He himself was a Bolshevik, but he was against the communists, and additionally he firmly ordered there to be calm. He would shoot on the spot anyone who robbed and killed.

At that moment a young Jewish boy came running to tell Moyshe that Klimenko's horsemen were destroying a Jewish store, and Moyshe whispered this to the ataman. Klimenko turned pale. He said that he had to leave immediately, and that the peasants should run the meeting without him. Klimenko left, and in less than half an hour he and his horsemen had left the shtetl.

17

A few days later five hundred men with a red flag and red bands on their hats came from the shtetl Torgovitsa to Dubova. They were all armed with rifles, and they carried machine guns with them. They were Red partisans from Yelisavetgrad district's well-known commercial center Novoarkhangelsk, located near the bridge over the Syniukha River, directly across from the shtetl Torgovitsa that is largely populated with Russian bastard merchants. These youth from the developed settlement of Great Russia on the border of Ukraine and New Russia were aligned with communism, and during the civil war of the summer of 1919 they stood on the side of the Moscow government. Of their own free will they went through the Jewish shtetls around Uman to eradicate the local bandits.

They also came to Dubova with that goal. Because Klimenko's horsemen also bore red flags and bands, the Jews of the shtetl were afraid of them. They immediately wanted to run to Moyshe the wheelwright for him to come to an agreement with them about a bribe, but at that minute Vasili Plakhotni, a Dubova peasant, a former Baltic fleet sailor and an indoctrinated communist, who, like the Jews, was hiding from the local and foreign bandits, arrived. He and his young Gentile woman would not leave the house without a gun. This particular Red comrade conversed briefly with the arriving partisans, and, upon learning whom they were looking for, quietly handed over the names of Brishko's relative, the Petliura officer Andrei Ovtsharuk, and the dark-haired sailor Petro Moniuno, who were both hard-working collaborators with Brishko himself.

At this time Ovtsharuk was already a civilian. He had gleefully participated in the killings in Uman but he came home an unhappy person. He foreswore doing any more work for the good of Ukraine and sat with his father and mother on the porch of their quaint white house with the two fragrant linden trees by the door and read a book.

Moniuno the sailor had managed to hide out, and they arrested Ovtsharuk with his book in hand. The Red Army partisans from the Russian bastard trading center of Novoarkhangelsk led him through the streets, deathly pale and bare-headed, and pointed two loaded revolvers at both of his ears. His father, the wealthy peasant Dezerye Ovtsharuk, who even in the previous years was a dangerous antisemite, ran after him and yelled, "Brothers, Jews, save my child! He is not doing anyone any harm! He is only sitting in the house with his books! Brothers, Jews, whoever believes in God, save him!"

A fear fell over the shtetl. He, Dezerye, was a violent old man, and Brishko and Andrei Ovtsharuk were close relatives. Their mothers were sisters, so Brishko would surely seek revenge for Andrei. And so the Jewish community decided to plead for Dezerye's "innocent" son. The wealthiest Jewish Dubova householders were pleading for him, and swore that he was not responsible for the Jewish killings. They forcefully dragged Moyshe the wheelwright out of his house to put in a good proletarian word for Andrei, that he was honestly not involved with anything and was truly just sitting at home with books.

The Red partisans asked the Dubova Jews not to interfere and not to do any favors for the bandits. Meanwhile they were quietly advised by the Red sailor Vasili Plakhotni not to listen to the Jews with their false antics, because they were cowards. But the wealthy Dubova Jewish householders were more determined. They kissed the hands of the Russian bastards of Novoarkhangelsk for so long until they gave up on them along with their arrestee and left town.

18

This particular incident with Andrei Ovtsharuk strongly affected Markela Brishko. If the Jews have such a great influence on the Bolsheviks, then "the game is for the devil." The Red punitive brigade had by then spread itself across the entire Uman area. One had to merely point out someone to get the Bolsheviks to point two loaded revolvers at both his ears. If this was the case, he, Markela, needed to know where he stood with the Dubova Jewish community.

And so he tested them.

One time, in the middle of the day, twenty unfamiliar armed horsemen with a red flag and red bands on their hats came to his residence in Korzhova, and they took Brishko with them in a wagon, bound hand and foot. They stopped near the volost, and someone announced that the Jews of the shtetl should gather together regarding a very important matter. Naturally the Jews immediately came running. The horsemen then displayed the arrested and bound Markela, and they asked the Jews whether he had done them any harm. If they were to say one word against him, the horsemen would shoot him to death, because they were from the Red punitive brigade that was rooting out the bandits.

The Jewish men of the community, encircled by women and children, listened, frightened and confused. A few elderly householders ran to get Moyshe the wheelwright, but before he arrived a few voices from the Jewish community called out with words of praise for the bound man. Moyshe as a proletarian confirmed this, and everybody started saying good things about the good local Markela, who protected the shtetl like his own life. No, the Dubova Jews had nothing against him, and they pleaded that no one do anything to harm him.

Then Brishko stood up and threw down the ropes that bound him. He immediately jumped down from the wagon and laughed loudly about his scheme. His soldiers laughed too at how they had fooled an entire shtetl of Jews, but the Jews themselves were blessing God for saving them from this danger.

After Brishko had tested the Dubova Jews he became calmer. He came to an agreement with Moyshe the wheelwright in a comradely manner about guarding the shtetl, and that the Jews should give him payments to maintain his partisans. He also had his own interests in mind. He needed to get married. Feyge-Vitele was there in Korzhova with the zemstvo teacher.

She already knew all the prayers, and still the priest did not want to convert her.

The Korzhova priest was very cautious in this matter. The Dubova story of Andrei Ovtsharuk, about whom the Jews begged the Bolsheviks to spare his life, made a deep impression on him. The Red punitive battalion was wandering around the entire region! At any time when their group was looking for bandits it could happen that the Jews would point him out, since he and Brishko were connected because he converted a Jewish girl for him. Also, priests were generally suspicious that they might shoot one of them for any little thing. He explained this very politely to Brishko and sent him to his colleague, the priest from Vilshanka. He lived farther from the shtetl, so it would be more comfortable for him to do this.

But the priest from Vilshanka did not want to convert Feyge-Vitele either. This was probably because of the same concern. But what he told Markela was that it would be difficult for him to do so, because her grandfather was a kosher meat tax collector and her father was a cantor. This meant that she was from a "spiritual calling." The Jews from Uman would really start talking about this, and this would trigger complaints to the metropolitan in Kyiv.

At such a time, converting a Jew was a very tricky thing, and therefore he suggested that it would be better if Markela traveled to Kurtenke. It was far away from the shtetl. The village was very small. There the priest would do this for him in one minute.

Brishko did as he asked. He did also take precautions for the priest of Kurtenke. Since his Fanya was from such a highly prominent family that the Jews from Uman could take vengeance for her, he needed to protect himself with an official note from the Dubova Jews that they had no complaints toward him about getting married to their cantor's daughter and their kosher meat tax collector's granddaughter.

He turned to Moyshe the wheelwright with this request. There he explained to him that Feyge-Vitele was going to change her religion of her own free will, and that they had been in love with each other for more than two years. Moyshe told him that he should write the note himself, that he should also indicate who should sign it. Brishko wrote it, and aside from him, Moyshe Shvartsman and Gedalye Koretsky, he named three other important householders in Dubova.

The five men signed the note and the Kurtenke priest accepted it, agreeing to convert the Jewish girl.

After the wedding the young couple remained living in the village of Korzhova where some of Brishko's partisans were located. He watched over the Dubova shtetl from there.

19

Brishko truly guarded the shtetl. When his soldiers came across Jews in the street, if anyone had a pair of decent boots, they would always take ownership of them. Often the soldiers would empty out their bags, and they were not stingy with a few good beatings at the same time. Brishko's co-workers from the Ukrainian authorities, the former sailors and the free thinkers who had traveled around the world, used to give speeches about Jews on Thursdays at the market, "In the past it was the notion that they were also human beings and that everyone was equal. Afterward the Jews lured everyone into a sack. But they never had time to tie up the sack, so we must protect ourselves with ax and scythe in hand."

A second person of this group, who during the time of the Bolsheviks ostensibly advocated free ideas and therefore Jews voted him onto all the committees, also used to hold forth about the Jewish people, but more politely. Using symbolism, he told about an old rotten tree that prevented all the surrounding saplings from growing, and how one had to tear out the tree by its roots.

But these were all just minor incidents that occurred among folks from town. Brishko really was standing guard. He would not allow out-of-town bandits into the shtetl, and this stirred great desire towards Dubova in the ataman bandit Kozakov.

Kozakov was also from the surrounding area of Uman. He came from the shtetl Mankovke. Years earlier a Gentile woman with a three-year-old child in her arms went there and got a job as a maid for the private lawyer Donetsky. She had come from Odesa with the child.

She worked for Donetsky for two years, and afterward she married the Mankovke peasant Kozakov. Her child took the stepfather's family name, and he grew up to be the notorious bandit Kozakov.

In Mankovke he studied in the two-grade zemstvo school along with many Jewish children from the shtetl. He was a big troublemaker in school, and so they expelled him from the third grade.

For a while he was unemployed and used to do odd jobs in Jewish homes. He loved most to carry chickens to the shochet to be slaughtered, but in time his mother's former boss, the lawyer Donetsky, hired him as a driver for the fire brigade that he organized in Mankovke. Afterward Kozakov became an assistant to the zemstvo doctor Zelinsky, but quickly he went back to Donetsky. This time he worked for him as a watchman in the beet fields.

During the war Kozakov was conscripted, and he went to serve in the army. He served in Odesa, but not for long: he fled from the army and became a deserter. He returned home to Mankovke and brought with him two revolvers and a rifle. He did not stay with his mother because he was afraid they would capture him. His stepfather was already dead. His mother was a merchant who earned money, and because of this she had many enemies among the neighboring peasants. She often used to travel to Odesa and would bring both fabric and ready-made clothes from there.

Until the Revolution started Kozakov hid from those who envied his mother. He was captured a few times. Bound up he was taken to Uman, and he would still escape. Ostrozhnik, his relative from a nearby village, always hid him.

After the Revolution, when an amnesty was declared for all deserters, Kozakov went back to the army. For a long time, no one heard from him. His mother used to tell the tale that he became a big military man in Odesa. There his bandit career also began.

It was April 1919, precisely when Petliura came to power. While coming out publicly against the Reds, Petliura immediately began his massacres of Jews. At the Great Fountain of Odesa he killed all the Jewish militiamen, and, accompanied by his followers, around sixty people, he marched on the Baltic road to Podilia, killing along the way the old and young in all the Jewish shtetls. This is how he killed the Jewish community of his home shtetl of Mankovke.

It was already in June when local peasant banditry had become an everyday occurrence in the Uman area. Every energetic Gentile youth from the village used to gather about ten of his friends, grab a red-colored rag from his mother, and turn it into a flag. They took up a few axes and pitchforks and marched through the shtetls killing Jews. Entire communities used to hide in their attics from these gangs of peasant youths. The most respectable people from the Ukrainian Jewish communities kissed their filthy hands and feet and ransomed their lives from them with wealth that they had scraped together for generations. The decent local peasants along with their wives and children stood around them doubled over with laughter. Mainly the audience loved the demeaning deaths devised by the Gentile youths for Jews. Later they were so popular among the peasant population that at the market they would make a sport of killing Jews, and the village youth ran to watch, as if they were attending an amazing circus act.

At this opportune time Kozakov arrived to his familiar Uman fields. The nearer he was to those from Uman, the more the Christian community showed support for him. The leaders were the students and teachers that were called by the noble name "Left SRs."[46] Meanwhile the Ukrainian yellow-blue flag fluttered over all the slaughters of Jews. In the name of the people's authority killing Jews was legal. Kozakov really was happy as a clam. He thought of casting off the shameful name "bandit" in favor of becoming a Ukrainian Republic "fighter-for-the-people," just as Klimenko and all of his comrades had done.

20

On the eve of Shavuot in the year 5679[47] Kozakov, with these important thoughts, went into Dubova with his "soldiers" with the purpose of discussing joint "work" in the community with Ataman Klimenko, who had already mobilized his peasant army in the surrounding villages.

Kozakov went into the shtetl with 150 men, all dressed as sailors with red bands on their hats and two red flags in their hands. The ataman himself wore a well-tailored French coat. They all stopped in the market and were scrutinizing the shtetl.

Moyshe the wheelwright immediately went to the volost to ask Smelnitski, the head of the People's authority, whether he knew who the newcomers were. He and Kopnik were already at that moment standing guard for the Dubova Jews because they had been paid well to do so.

"They call themselves Red Sailors," Smelnitski answered, "but they are not such good sailors ..."

Meanwhile the ataman with the French coat arrived, and together all three of them[48] went to a peasant's tavern. Later Moyshe also went there. They were sitting at the table and drinking vodka. When Moyshe was left standing at the door, the ataman said that he could come in, but he answered that he needed the village leader. Smelnitski went out into the yard to Moyshe and told him that he was demanding a Jewish deputation.

Moyshe immediately ran to Gedalye Koretsky, but he wasn't home, so in the street he grabbed an old man, someone named Sholem Daytshman, and went back to the tavern with him.

As before, the three of them were sitting around a flask of vodka. Ataman Kozakov looked from under his brow at the two Jews and asked them if they knew who this army was.

To this Moyshe tactically and cautiously answered, "We know from the village leader that they are Bolsheviks and are active against the communists. The Jews agree with this and we want to help those who are fighting for the people."

The ataman looked at his wristwatch, and he itemized word by word that within a half hour they should bring him 25,000 rubles, a half a pood of sausages, oats for the horses, and lunch and vodka for the soldiers.

Moyshe told Smelnitski to give the "soldiers" what they needed and to put it on his account, and he himself, along with the deputy that he grabbed, ran back to the shtetl looking for people and called everyone to a meeting in the small synagogue. The people immediately assembled and in the blink of an eye collected the 25,000 rubles. Everyone gave whatever they had at home.

But as they were handing over the money, there was a misfortune. The old man Sholem Daytshman had a notion to beg the ataman to take less because people living in the shtetl were poor. The ataman got very angry, his face became red, and his blond messed-up clump of hair became messier. He hurled the money back at them shouting, "Save yourselves, whoever can! I am going to burn down the shtetl!"

Moyshe started to beg him not to base his actions on the words of an old man. The two local Christians[49] also asked him, and it didn't help. But at that moment a short, dark-haired sailor with small shifty eyes called Moyshe out to the yard and told him quietly to remain calm. The ataman would take the money. He, the dark-haired one, would persuade him.

Meanwhile everybody went out into the street, the dark-haired one with Ataman Kozakov in front and the others behind them. Along the way they went into a peasant's house. There the ataman agreed to take the money. He counted it, rejecting three fifties, and also noted a missing 500, and once again the old Sholem Daytshman interjected that the ataman may have made a mistake in counting. With these words the ataman once again rejected the money. But Moyshe did not lose his composure. He began to explain that the old man was sleepy and so he was talking nonsense. In the end the ataman took the money, and he ordered the old man to get out of his sight. He also demanded five flasks of vodka. Moyshe immediately brought him the vodka and the 500-note, and the ataman gave his word that his "soldiers" would not touch anything in the shtetl.

The night passed calmly. The ruling committee realized that this was due to Kozakov, and they also informed Moyshe of this. Ataman Kozakov and his soldiers spent the night in the village, and it was like a holiday. He bestowed the gold and silver of the Jews upon the young peasants, and in every house there was a festive meal with harmonicas, singing, and dancing. But the dark-haired sailor wasn't there with them. Until the evening he was sitting with Moyshe in his house. He ate supper with him, and, while sitting at the table, he disclosed in great secrecy that he was a Jewish child from Odesa. He and the ataman had once been arrested for a robbery, and from then on they were good friends. Now he accompanied him to be an intermediary for Jews. In this way he saved entire shtetls from death. Moyshe was afraid to ask a lot, and he praised him for the good that he was doing for Jews.

In the morning Kozakov went to Babanka to discuss "working" with Klimenko as a unified force. But Klimenko sharply answered that he shot bandits on the spot, and that he had already ordered him to be arrested. But Kozakov was able to run away to another village and hid there.

Meanwhile in Dubova there was mayhem. In the late morning, when Kozakov's "Red" sailors wanted to follow him to Babanka along with the peasant youth from the village streets who had joined up with their ataman the previous night, a Jew from Dubova, Zekharye Kozodoy, had a notion to accuse the local murderers who killed his two small children in the butcher Dovid Furman's house on the first night of the Dubova killings.

It was the first day of Shavuot. Men in their long cloth cloaks and women dressed in silk were coming out of the synagogues. Upon coming out of the small synagogue Zekharye saw sailors with red flags and was certain that they were Bolsheviks. So he approached them and told them about the great heinous deed that local people had done to him.

Immediately there was a loud noise around him. An agitated mob ran out from the peasant streets, encircling Zekharye to lynch him on the spot, because he had accused the village in front of out-of-town people. It was a miracle that these "Reds" were not Bolsheviks. Otherwise they would have immediately put loaded revolvers to both ears of every single person that Zekharye Zhid pointed out.

But Zekharye stood among the angry peasant crowd, a bloodied man with a torn-out beard, and shouted that he had to bring to justice these murderers who killed his two innocent children.

Upon hearing this, strong peasant hands responded with blows from every side. Jewish men and women in holiday clothes, with prayer books and prayer shawls in their hands, were standing around him and begging for mercy. In the same way that they, the Jews, had begged for the life of Dezerye's son from the Red Russian bastards of Novoarkhangelsk, they now begged for pity on Zekharye. "He is a father, his life is bitter because of the death of his children, so he is speaking from his heart. The Jews of the shtetl guarantee that he will not do any harm to the locals." But the begging and pleading was heard by no one. A dull rasping roar resounded in the air, everywhere there were red angry faces and clenched fists. Above their heads their axes and knives gleamed in the sun.

But at this moment a miracle happened. A cannon shot was heard, and the rat-a-tat of a machine gun and the crackling of gunshots began from the direction of Korzhova. It was Klimenko who was shooting at Kozakov and his bandits, and coming in from the other direction were Brishko and his partisans. This is how the peasant streets were caught between two blasts of gunfire. The angry mob let go of the fainted Zekharye and set off running for the bridge. The "Red" sailors ran off somewhere, and the two peasant youths who had joined with Kozakov the night before took off their white embroidered shirts and raised them into the air on sticks as a sign that they were surrendering.

The shooting immediately stopped. Brishko and his partisans came into Dubova and disarmed the few "Red" uniformed sailors that remained in the shtetl. He also confiscated the weapons that Kozakov had given the peasant youth the night before, and on that same day, in accordance with Klimenko's orders, Kozakov himself was arrested and brought to Klimenko's house in Babanka. Klimenko ordered Kozakov to be shot in the morning at sunrise.

But the incited Babanka peasants were by now stronger than the Ukrainian left "SR" Klimenko. In the evening his own soldiers freed Kozakov and let him run to wherever his heart desired. He went to the surrounding villages where he met many of his sailors, and he went with them to Dubova to unite with the village youth that he had armed there.

Kozakov stopped near the telephone station and went to see the telephone operator Yelena Vasiliyevna, whom he had met and befriended the first time he was there. His "sailors" were now without red bands on their hats. Upon encountering the first militiaman passing by, they told him to go tell the dark-haired Jew who always treated soldiers to food that they were hungry. So he went and told Moyshe the wheelwright who immediately showed up with bread, sausages, and vodka. Along with the militiaman they all went to the volost, and there they sat down to eat.

However, someone began firing upon the shtetl at that moment, and this made Brishko aware that Kozakov was once again in Dubova, and Brishko and his partisans crossed the bridge to catch him dead or alive.

But the Dubova peasants pulled the same thing on Brishko that was done in the village of Babanka to Ataman Klimenko. By the time Markela had taken the guns away from Kozakov's five "soldiers," who were still armed and sitting in the volost at lunch provided by Moyshe the wheelwright and the Jewish community, Kozakov had disappeared somewhere. He was being hidden by the hunchback old maid Yelena Vasiliyevna, with whom a romance had blossomed. When Brishko went looking for Kozakov in the telephone station, the bandit was already hidden in her room, inside a wardrobe between hanging clothes and coats. Yelena said directly to Markela that Kozakov had run out through the window into the yard. Dimitri Shabolinski, the owner of the house, also verified this.

Dimitri was actually one of the "free thinkers." During the time of Kerensky he served in the military, but, when the army at the front fled home, he came to Dubova with the free ideas of a Bolshevik. He was a rich peasant with land and was a good shoemaker. He also dealt in pigs and built for himself the two nicest houses in Dubova. Before marriage, his wife Tolia Shabolinski was a maid in Jewish houses. She also worked for the rebbetzin for a long time. She also sold all sorts of goods in the markets. Both were very friendly with Jews, both spoke Yiddish, and Tolia's Yiddish expressions were charming.

On the night of the massacre on the second day of Pesach many Jewish families hid at Dimitri's. Yet this same Dimitri helped Yelena, the disabled "daughter" of the dark and thirsty-for-predation Uman district, save the life of the ataman bandit Kozakov. It may have been that Dimitri feared revenge from the people of the village who saw Kozakov as one of their own, standing for the peasants and acting against the Zhids. But it was more likely that he just didn't want any shootings in his house and shattering of the big windows of the telephone station, and therefore he hid Kozakov well. When Markela surrounded Dimitri's yard with guards and he himself went into the house to search all the corners, Yelena Vasiliyevna then led Kozakov down to the cellar through the back door so he could crawl into an empty barrel there and throw a few sacks over the top.

Brishko searched everywhere. He threatened Shabolinski that he would burn his house down and that his entire property would disappear in flames. But he swore on his life that Kozakov was not there. He even sent him to search the cellar. Markela had already opened it but he hesitated ... At that point he trusted Dimitri's word. Dimitri Shabolinski was a free-thinking person. One couldn't believe that he would hide bandits in his house.

21

Kozakov stayed at Dimitri Shabolinski's late into the night, and, when the last fire was extinguished in the Jewish houses, Dimitri took him on a ride into the fields so that he could flee into the wide world in order that Markela's eye would not be able to find him. But Kozakov did not run far. He gathered "soldiers" in the nearby villages Nebelivka and Oksanyna and went with them to Torgovitsa, twenty-five versts from Dubova.

And there a miracle happened.

The dark-haired Jewish sailor, who had befriended Kozakov when they were both arrested for theft in Odesa, came from that shtetl. During the big turmoil, when Klimenko started to fire a cannon at Kozakov's "sailors," he ran home to his elderly father and mother who thought that he had been killed somewhere during the war.

In a few days Kozakov arrived in Torgovitsa with his new "soldiers," and there he ran into his Jewish sailor friend. He began to beg Kozakov in his usual manner not to do anything bad to this shtetl, as here lived poor Jews and tradesmen who were maintaining themselves with their own ten fingers. Meanwhile he told Kozakov about his elderly father and mother who were crying their eyes out waiting for him. Afterward he went with Kozakov to the river and showed him the place near the bridge where he as a child used to dive into the underwater depths. Also, he showed him the peasant fields with the high prickly hedges where he used to climb on dark nights stealing apples. And as a result of this Kozakov did this favor for him. Kozakov allowed the Jews of Torgovitsa to live, but he demanded a contribution of 60,000 rubles from them.

And when the Red Russian bastards of the trade district of Novoarkhangelsk located across the river from the shtetl Torgovitsa heard of this, they sent a message in secret to the

Jews in the shtetl that they better not dare give any contribution to the bandits, because they, the Red Russian bastards, would deal with this in another way. And if they did not obey, then the members of the district would come and destroy the entire shtetl.

Kozakov and his "soldiers" meanwhile crossed the bridge into Novoarkhangelsk. It was already evening. The militia from the district welcomed them very nicely. They immediately gave them a place to sleep in a big house which was formerly a dance hall. Later many young people came there. They began to drink with the newcomers in a brotherly manner. They celebrated like this until late in the night, and, when they were good and drunk, someone threw a bomb at them which killed fourteen people. The rest of them ran into the dark fields, and Kozakov himself was also lucky to escape with his life.

22

It was quiet in Dubova from the second day of Shavuot, when Brishko drove out Kozakov, until the 20th of Sivan.[50] During this period the shtetl was only frightened by Muzhilinski, the former spy of the ataman. The spy was unemployed, so he gathered a few young men from several outlying areas of Uman and with them went looking for "luck" in the nearby Jewish shtetls. They were very few in number and looked like city people. They went through the village streets dressed in city clothes, with new accessories, yellow shoes, and the caps that they had pillaged in the days of the Uman massacre, and the peasant youth began to laugh at them. They did rob a few Jewish stores, and Moyshe the wheelwright bargained with them to take a contribution of 15,000 rubles ... in the midst of the strong laughter of the peasant community they quietly and shamefully left the shtetl, and the Jewish community thanked God for delivering them from danger.

At this time Brishko was seldom seen in Dubova. He was completely focused on his own private affairs. After his change of heart during the Jewish killings in Uman, his friend Andrei Ovtsharuk, the Petliura officer, settled in at his father and mother's house and sat over a book, and Brishko was busy with Feyge-Vitele. After the wedding Feyge-Vitele became very interested in sports. Brishko taught her how to ride a bicycle and to ride on the small slim ponies that were only to be found in the surrounding villages. One could always encounter them riding on the Uman highway, quietly smiling and happily in love.

In the shtetl one would only see the *"atamaness"* in the market. Fayge-Vitele would arrive wearing attractive colored glass pearls and ribbons and a red jacket with embroidered sleeves, just like the Ukrainian peasant daughters. She never met with any Jews. She also avoided her grandfather's house, but in the shtetl it was said that once, between day and night, she came from Korzhova on her bicycle and rode into her grandfather Shkodnik's yard. She called Etele out to tell her to ask her grandparents whether she could come in and see them. And Khaye actually agreed to it, but Shmuel-Yitskhok firmly ordered her not to dare cross his threshold.

He, Shmuel-Yitskhok Shkodnik, did not want to see anyone in these last days. Since the morning after the second night of massacres, when Etele told him the news that Fanya, Feyge-Vitele, got married to Markela, he became hunched over, and thought of himself as small and unworthy. He stopped giving his opinions in the shtetl community, became disinterested in any business, and he removed himself completely from the world. His comfortable joyous home that had sparkled with the happiness and song of young girls was now bleak. Etele moved around melancholically, pining for Andriusha whom she loved. Andrei also loved her, but he would seldom come by because his father Dezerye Ovtsharuk would not allow it. He soon threatened to disinherit him if he were to commit an abominable act like Markela did and marry Shkodnik's zhid girl Etele. Etele's other good friends from the Dubova Christian community also avoided visiting her at her Jewish grandfather's house. They all became somewhat angry and silently nasty to her. The feldsher Deviatkin often showed his cynical hatred of Jews, and in the zemstvo hospital he mimicked the faces of wounded Jews who were brought there with hacked limbs during the days of the Dubova massacre. The quiet and polite midwife Shnuruk also became more talkative. She would tell her Jewish women in childbirth about the type of bargains she bought from Kozakov's "sailors." She also "consoled" them that there would be "news": they would again slaughter young and old.

At this time the Red Terror of the Moscow punitive brigade reigned in the Ukrainian villages, and at the same time the Black Army[51] of the counterrevolution strengthened itself. The latter painted themselves all over in the national colors and were united in the idea of exterminating the Jewish people. By that time also marching under the Ukrainian flag were the half-witted Russians, who had been the administrators of the government institutions of the old order, and who afterward were left without a leg to stand on or a way to make a living. The ignorant sons of the rich Russians hid under the yellow-blue colors too, as did the dull bloodthirsty officer class of the old Russian state. In this way the national flag of the Ukrainian Peasant Republic paved the way for the oncoming black Tatar Denikin's[52] army, with its black terror, black drunken killings of Jews, and black Russian patriotism, to enslave once again all the nations of the former Great Russia.

Kozakov's bandit army was composed of this diverse set of elements when he attacked the Dubova shtetl for the second time.

23

It was Tuesday, the 20th of Sivan,[53] on a rainy early morning.

The shtetl was unprotected at that time. Klimenko and the voluntary military groups he organized in the villages had left for Uman to fight the iron might of the Bolsheviks, and Brishko had become a private citizen. Brishko was totally busy with

Feyge-Vitele and her sport activities. His partisans, whom the Dubova Jews were feeding, were leaderless and also became private citizens, and even the few militiamen from the shtetl had no duties or responsibilities to anyone. The only remaining defenders of the Dubova Jews were the two former sailors Kopnik and Smelnitski, who represented the administration of the peasant authorities. They, the former "free thinkers" who had become sympathizers of the Ukrainian national movement, helped Moyshe the wheelwright negotiate with the ataman of the bandits each time to spare the lives of the Dubova Jews.

In this instance there was no time for negotiations. Kozakov was in a hurry because Soviet troops were waiting at the Uman train station for the arrival from the nearby Khrystynivka station of the Red armored car, which used to instill fear in all the bandits. Therefore Kozakov acted quickly. The massacre lasted two hours in total. Altogether fifteen people were killed, aside from the wounded and injured, who remained permanently disabled. But these violent and humiliating deaths were so gruesome that the night of the massacre on Pesach Sheni perpetrated by the local people wearing the inside-out jackets seemed like child's play.

Kozakov was still dressed in his finely-woven democratic French coat, which served him as a reminder of his first sunny happy revolutionary days in Odesa. His two colleagues, the bandit leaders, appeared modestly dressed in rubber jackets and small sports caps over their brows. They were the rich peasant Shevchenko, who in his home village of Takshi became a great bon vivant, and the former seminarian Popov from Tiraspol, with his heroic past as a flaming Red Bolshevik. Aside from the three elegant democratic-like atamans, many "intellectual" faces of sons born to wealth also stood out. They were dressed in fancy English suits and expensive raincoats with hoods over their heads.

Popov brought with him from the Dniester shore a union of three gangs from Ukraine, Great Russia, and Moldova. They brought with them two hundred empty wagons, one hundred horsemen, almost four hundred infantry, a few machine guns, and a cannon. They entered Dubova with music and red banners. The slogan on the lead banner read "Peace for the Houses of the Poor and War on the Palaces!" but a red silk banner also fluttered nearby with the slogan, "Death to the Jews and Save Russia!" Someone also dragged along a yellow-blue flag of the Ukrainian Republic.

During a rainstorm they stopped in the middle of the market, and Moyshe the wheelwright immediately got to work. Highly motivated, he tore through the rows of the ruling committee to the two advocates for the Jews, Smelnitski and Kopnik, entreating them to do something. But they dropped their hands. Both nodded with their heads, "They are coming, it appears, only to take lives. The ataman ordered all Jewish men to gather in the synagogue for a 'meeting,' but we heard from the 'soldiers' that they wanted to trick the Jews into going there and then burn down the synagogue." They told Moyshe this in secret, and immediately they entreated him to run home to his wife and child. They themselves would let everyone know not to go to the synagogue. In truth, when Smelnitski and Kopnik went out the door, a few frightened Jews were running into the small synagogue because the soldiers had summoned everyone to go there to speak with the ataman. Smelnitski firmly ordered the Jews to stay at home, but at that moment an old Gentile woman approached them and pointed out the orchards and gardens where they should escape. At the same time she made the sign of the cross and said quietly, "Heathens ... they are already killing ...."

Moyshe grabbed a militiaman by his hand and ran back with him through the rows of bandits. When he came home, he and his eldest son, the beloved coddled Khananye, went to work together on the wheels in his workshop. His wife and their small children remained sitting in the house by the sewing machine, and Moyshe told her to keep treadling and to continue sewing without stopping.

Meanwhile the bandits found a place to organize themselves. They rode into the big yard of the zemstvo post office, where there were fine stalls for horses and large covered stables for the wagons, and they established a very nice headquarters on the top floor in the beautiful apartment of Yankl Feldman, the owner of the house and the person leasing out the post office. Luckily, Yankl and his family ran away from Dubova in time, and the apartment was empty. But below this there was another apartment, where old Getsl Portigul lived with his wife and stepdaughter Sosye. And this particular lower floor with its windows at ground level was a place of refuge to hide during all the catastrophes. His children, grandchildren, relatives, and good friends from the shtetl would immediately run to old Getsl.

This time too, that's how it went. Even before the bandits rode into the post office yard, the lower apartment of Getsl Portigul was already full of people, and there was no time to run, because as soon as the bandits arrived, they stationed two guards at the gate with their unsheathed swords held high to watch the entrance.

The bandits immediately divided into groups and went around to the Jewish houses. There they ordered all drawers and chests be opened, and from each Jewish house they took the best and most valuable possessions. They also dragged every single Jew they saw into the headquarters with them.

Immediately the bandits drove the Jews' cows into the post office yard to be slaughtered. With whips in their hands they also chased Jewish girls and women into the headquarters to cook the fresh meat of the Jews' butchered cattle, serve the officers, and make merry with the soldiers ... This is how they dragged everyone, numbly petrified and hysterically screaming, up to the top floor, beating them with sticks and whips, and they chopped off limbs from the men and threw them down into the cellar which was situated near the gate to the yard.

This massacre transpired very quietly. The leader was the tall, robust seminarian Popov from Tiraspol himself. He firmly ordered all the bandits to save gunpowder and to kill everyone with cold steel. This order was obeyed immediately. No one was able to obtain a bullet with any amount of pleading. Also, according to his orders Jewish women were raped, but all their lives were spared. As Popov stood over the killings next to the post office cellar, he issued orders like a military man. But he did not allow any Ukrainian peasant youth to do this noble "work." They only packed the stolen goods into the wagons, and the Russians and Moldovans stood by the door to the cellar with axes and swords. For every victim that was brought, he ordered to a beat, "One—pick up the saber, two—pick up the saber, hack away! ...."

The Gentile horsemen of the zemstvo post office also pointed out to Popov the apartment of Getsl Portigul on the lower floor, where there were always many Jews hiding.

The bandits stormed into the apartment and immediately dragged all the girls from there up into the headquarters. They killed old Getsl's son-in-law Yeshaye Daytshman before his very eyes. In the meantime, they ordered his wife Dvoyre Daytshman to sit and watch how they killed her husband. He was the handsome Dubova householder whom Moyshe previously, a month earlier, took along as an embellishment in the deputation to Klimenko. This time they chopped off his fingers and toes, and with every chop they would sing along in Russian, "This would have been a nice Commissar!"

Yeshaye's eighteen-year-old son Dudik Daytshman escaped from the house with a hacked-up throat and neck, and ran into the village to the mocking laughter of the curious Gentile men and women, but a peasant boy who sat on the same bench with him in the zemstvo school grabbed him and turned him back over to the bandits. The "merciful" sister who accompanied the united bandit army put him out of his misery with a sword, pushing the dead body away from them into a rain gutter.

Afterward they went after Getsl himself. He was already an old man of seventy, bent over and weak, and so he begged them to let him live. He wanted to see his children in America. He was not going to stay in Ukraine, he would travel to his son on the other side of the ocean, and the thieves granted the old Jew his life. But meanwhile there was a misfortune with his beautiful stepdaughter, and because of this he had to pay with his life.

This was Sosye, his wife's youngest daughter from her first husband, for whom the refined woman Basye Portigul scrimped bits of food from her own mouth so that her daughter could go to the Uman gymnasium and complete all six grades. On the 20th of Sivan of 5679,[54] Sosye was twenty-two years old. She was tall and glowing with blond braids, large blue eyes, and a clear, pale face. When they dragged her up into the headquarters, a fight immediately broke out among the bandits, each one grabbing her to himself. With blood-flushed faces they started stabbing each other with their swords. Sosye was standing between them with two black eyes. Wildly disheveled and dumbfounded, she let herself be dragged from all sides by their strong hands. They tore her clothes off, pulled out her braids, and they pinched her dazzling white body many times until it bled. Then they threw themselves with iron fists at each other's beat-up chests.

In the end it was resolved that they would shoot her to death. "If one of us doesn't get her, no one will." They would shoot her right there on the spot. And afterward they would throw her under the stables, and the ataman would not know anything about it. But while the agitated bandit youths were deciding what to do with the Jewish girl, hitting each other in the heads with the handles of their guns, a short Moldovan sailor took Sosye by the hand and led her out the door.

"Promise me that you will convert and marry me, and I will save you ... They will immediately shoot you, and they will throw you to the dogs."

This is what the short Moldovan with the thick lips said to her and the numb Sosye nodded her head. Then he quietly led her down the stairs. He left the yard with her unnoticed by the ataman and his bandits, who were occupied near the killing cellar, and then he brought her to a peasant's house in a Gentile street, asking them to watch over the Jewish girl for a few days because she was his bride. In a few days he would come for her and bring her to the church, and then he immediately disappeared from the shtetl.

Meanwhile in the headquarters they realized that the Jewish girl had slipped through their fingers, so the bandits started to run down into the yard to search for her. But the young horsemen of the post office, who were standing idly by the gate watching the violent deaths near the open doors of the cellar, had seen a short Moldovan sailor lead Sosye from the yard. They speculated that probably the old devil from the first floor had paid the sailor well for this, because she was his daughter.

These words ignited a hellfire there. A wild roar shook the air like the cry of a wolf, and a band of angry men ran down to the first floor like animals to take revenge on the old Jew for his beautiful daughter whom he took right out of their hands. This is how the little old man Getsl Portigul was once again dragged out to his death. On the stairs of the cellar they cut him with swords, chopping off both of his hands on a board for making noodles which was hanging on the cellar wall.

24

But during the day of the massacre on the 20th of Sivan, great miracles happened in Dubova.

On the massacre nights during the month of May the inside-out jacket-wearing locals bypassed the rabbi's house, and another miracle happened this time.

A few bandits broke into the rabbi's house but did not harm anyone. The rabbi himself was by then weak from old age and sick from Jewish woes. So he was lying in bed. The elderly energetic rebbetzin had been caring for him, calling the doctor from time to time for him, and regularly got all sorts of drops from the pharmacy to strengthen his heart. Kozakov's bandits ordered him to get out of bed because they had to search it to see whether he was hiding arms there.

The rabbi told the rebbetzin, "Tell them in their language that I am sick and cannot get up," and the elderly beautiful savvy woman began to beg them in their language. She showed them the bottles of drops that she got for him from the pharmacy and that she only had a 100-Nikolai bill, so she gave them the 100 as a bribe.

The bandits gave the money back to her. With the pale suffering old man lying in bed like a heap of bones they searched the house thoroughly, and they left the rabbi's house quietly.

The second miracle happened to Dovid Furman the butcher.

On the particular massacre night of Pesach Sheni, the bandits had killed six people in his house. His wife Zlata and his two small children were left disabled for their entire lives. Nonetheless people ran into the narrow street to him in order for him to hide them in his house. His neighbor from the market told him simply that he wanted to die within Furman's four walls. At this moment Zlata was lying in bed post-childbirth, and the neighbor grabbed the little pillow with the infant and began to beg that he wanted to hold it in his arms, as maybe the bandits would by the virtue of the innocent baby, allow him to remain alive. But another neighbor also wanted to benefit from the virtue of the child, so he begged Furman to give him the baby to hold from time to time—and God had mercy on Furman's house. This time they all begged for their lives from the bandits that tore in, and only one of them was a violent person. He specifically wanted to cut off Zlata's earrings along with her ears. But the other bandits were local Gentiles from the surrounding villages who took pity on her that she would lose her ears, so they stood up against him saying that he should take the earrings without the ears, and these bandits only took the boots from the two neighbors who were clinging to the pillow with the tiny child.

But the biggest miracle happened to the beautiful and honorable householder of Dubova, Yoysef Solodovnik.

The bandits who attacked his house killed his oldest son, Leyb Solodovnik, who had come from Bogopil with his wife and child to hide at his father's in Dubova. They hacked off some limbs from Leyb's body, forcing the old father and mother to sit on chairs and watch. They were also forced to watch them rape their fourteen-year-old daughter. While this was happening, the younger son came running with a quart of water to revive his fainted little sister, and because of this the bandits also wanted to kill him before the eyes of the old father and mother, but in that moment they heard the sounds of a trumpet horn, and the murderers ran from the house.

This was a signal to leave the shtetl.

At that point, small groups of peasants gathered in the Dubova market. While helping the out-of-town bandits rob the Jewish stores, the peasants were also making fun of the dancing of the crazy old maid Mindl Posternak. She was always kept locked away, but, at the moment when her old father and younger brother were dragged to the killing cellar, she ran out into the street and began dancing in front of the bandits.

She was very entertaining to them, so they got her drunk on vodka and accompanied her on the harmonica, throwing sweets at her that they had taken from the Jewish stores to pack in their wagons. But they had to leave everything behind and get themselves on the road. The Red armored car, whom the Uman Jews called the "Savior Angel," frightened everyone with a second signal heard in the air coming from the nearby station Khrystynivka, and the bandits left the shtetl accompanied by music and song from the village youth.

25

A Gentile woman banged on Moyshe the wheelwright's window, where his frightened children were clinging to their mother at the whirring sewing machine. She called upon Moyshe to go out to save people. Nobody wanted to go down into the cellar, they were afraid …

This happened immediately after the bandits left the Gentile streets. It was already quiet in the market, the crazy Mindl Posternak was sleeping next to a granary, leaning her head against a wet wall, and the peasant children were scrounging by the stores with the broken-down doors, looking to grab something for themselves and flee.

A sizeable group of Gentile men and women were standing by the killing cellar, and near them the Jewish wives and children were lamenting. The peasant voices yelled down, "Whoever is alive come out! Show yourself, whoever is alive! ... it is quiet now ..." and upon hearing this the Jewish women wailed into the dark void of the underground house of death.

A few Jews came out of their hiding places. Ukelman's widow ran out wringing her hands looking for her only son, Omtsenyu. The bandits had taken the Dubova prodigy Omtsenyu to their headquarters. They did not touch anything in his mother's house, but they tore Omtsenyu, the young, gentle bright Torah student, away from the open Gemara.

But here came Moyshe the wheelwright. He would soon find everybody. A miracle happened for him too: during the entire time of the massacre a Gentile stood by the door of his workshop, shouting out that they made very good wheels for the Russian Orthodox people here. It was as if, for the sake of the entire shtetl, he was a messenger from God. The lamenting women encircled Moyshe for him to do something. Who would go down into the cellars, if not him? In fact nobody budged from their spot. Jews and Gentiles, clinging together from fear, were standing by the open dark entry, and Moyshe the wheelwright did not lose his composure.

He was the first to put his foot on the ladder, and other strong-hearted people followed after him. The women with their cries and pleas to God also became brave. But immediately upon stepping on the dead people's hacked-up bodies and individual torn-off limbs, they jumped back out with a spasmic shudder, and once again wild wailings rang through the air.

Meanwhile two more strong-hearted men arrived. They went down into the cellar with candles in their hands, and immediately Moyshe the wheelwright was seen with a bloodied dead body on his shoulders.

Everyone was taken out; everyone was laid out in a row for identification. The wounded looked terrifyingly like sacks of broken bones. They stammered a few words and begged for help. A shudder passed through the rows of curious Gentile men and women who were standing by the open killing cellar. Mute and frightened they made the sign of the cross and asked for mercy from God, as if they were afraid of God's punishment and revenge, and one by one they silently left the place of the corpses.

And Ukelman's widow was still looking for her only son, the prodigy. She continuously cried out about a white shirt, saying that there wasn't one like it in the cellar. So she ran to Moyshe the wheelwright for him to go down there once more with her so they could keep looking among the barrels. And indeed in the darkness from behind a big barrel they heard a live creature breathing with difficulty and as they went closer with a lamp, they saw a person sitting with his head split open and gouged-out eyes, but he was still alive.

"It is Omtsenyu!" Moyshe's voice quivered with tears.

But the mother was unable to recognize him. She once more cried out about a white shirt that he was wearing, and this particular living corpse with the gouged-out eyes was wearing a red one ... In that moment she saw a white piece of sleeve from this blood-stained shirt, and she recognized it. She ran to her son, and she embraced his broken bones, crying, "Omtsenyu, Omtsenyu," but he couldn't speak. From the cellar they carried out a sack of bones wearing a red bloodied shirt.

The burial was two days later in the evening, because they were afraid to go to the cemetery beforehand. Smelnitski and Kopnik, the two protectors of the Jewish community, had received news that new bandits were wanting to attack Dubova. But on the next day an elderly Jew went from house to house, banging on the broken-down doors for them to bring the dead to the Jewish cemetery because of the great heat: it posed a danger to the living.

And between day and night, in the summer dusk with its thick smell of fields and gardens, a damp smell of corpses swept over the shtetl, and the Dubova Jewish community stole out to the cemetery with the murder victims and they were buried in silence.

But it was destined that on the third day they had to deal with yet another burial. The elderly Getsl Portigul had been buried with one hand because they couldn't find the other. But on the next morning Basye Portigul gave her potatoes from the killing cellar to a Gentile woman who then found the hand among the potatoes. A minyan of Jews carried the hand to the cemetery. They asked for forgiveness from Getsl, and his hand was buried separately.

26

A few days after the "small" massacre of the 20th of Sivan, two representatives of the Russian Red Cross came to Dubova and called together people of the community, Jews and Christians, to establish a committee that would find ways of getting food to the victims of the violence. However, the Jews of the shtetl refused to participate on any committee. They did not want to be involved anywhere. And they had no decent Christian who was better to be their representative than the shoemaker Dimitri Shabolinski. Even after he hid Kozakov he was still considered a person with "free" thinking, and at the time he was the only Christian in Dubova who still did a good deed for a Jew.

Everybody was helpless.

After the cellar massacre, the life of the Dubova Jews became totally paralyzed. Nobody wanted to open their shops; nobody worried about making a living. As usual Thursday in the market was bustling and noisy, but the Jews were afraid to show themselves in the outside world, because every Jewish misfortune began in the markets. Only the women were able to brace themselves and get out into the street to shop for the Shabbos. But they were more dead than alive. They were not cooking any lunch, and they couldn't bring themselves to clean up the destroyed houses. The few remaining possessions that had escaped the bandits' hands were buried in the cellars. Everything was packed up. Everything was ready for flight. There was an air of desolation. At night they slept in their clothes, all their relatives and friends gathered under one roof, and the day frightened them with pain and misery. A depression fell upon them, the news from everywhere made them insane. There was nowhere to run …

In Ladyzhynka the local murderers killed everybody. A hunchbacked shoemaker and a blind blacksmith were the only ones they left alive. On their joyous Sundays the locals made merry with the two disabled Jews and forced them both to dance and sing the Russian "Dubinushka,"[55] and for this they were to be given the Soviet money that they, the locals peasants, did not even want to touch.

And in Ternivka in broad daylight Kozakov slaughtered young and old. Every day the hunchbacked telephone operator of Dubova, Yelena Vasiliyevna, spoke with her beloved Kozakov by telephone. He sent regards to the Dubova Jews, and each time she told her dear friend, the quiet and shrewd midwife Shnuruk, that he would come visit Dubova again, and he would leave behind as many dead as in Kryve Ozero.[56] The Jews had three weeks to bury their dead after that, and Kozakov was going to kill from old to newborn. Most importantly, they had to kill the Jewish boys. Once they grew up, they would all become communists.

After the "small" massacre it suddenly became difficult for the Jewish pharmacist of Dubova, who in all his years was friends with Christian antisemites, to remain a Jew. So his good friend, the Vilshanka priest, did him a favor and converted him along with his wife and child. But before he became a Christian, he had to pay 10,000 Kerensky rubles to the Dubova Jewish community.

This was a double tax that the shtetl imposed on him which went into the bandit-fund, and he, while sitting in the wagon on the way to the conversion, had to pay it off immediately. Moyshe the wheelwright grabbed the horse by the bridle, and the Gentile wagon driver stuck up for the pharmacist. Then a few other Gentiles came to help the pharmacist, but the other side did not remain quiet either. A group of Jews encircled the wagon with the pharmacist. At this moment, while he was still a Jew, he had to pay the debts that were due to the Jewish community.

But it was Mitka Plakhotni, the famous thief and robber of the Dubova village, who collected the community debt from the pharmacist, because to the Bolsheviks Mitka was a communist and so by law was permitted to take from others. He listened to the claims from both sides, and on the spot declared that the community of Jews was right, and that the pharmacist had to pay the money.

Mitka ruled as such, and so the pharmacist settled his community debt. For that reason, the Dubova Jews still invited the pharmacist to hide in Jewish attics, just like the new converts in Uman did because their Christian neighbors would not accept them since they had changed their God.

And this blessing came true. After the conversion, the Dubova pharmacist had to entrust his Jewish pharmacy to the protection of the Christian cooperative. To hide his Jewish nose he needed to take in a Christian pharmacist. His wife and child remained living in Vilshanka under the pious custody of the priest, and, when the bandits attacked the Dubova shtetl, the converted pharmacist regrettably had to run to Vilshanka by himself by way of the orchards to benefit from the protection of the priest's holy wings.

Also, at that time the Dubova lawyer Nestrovsky was frightened by his Jewishness, so he also sought help in Vilshanka. But it was very difficult for the elderly lawyer to simply go to the church, so the priest did him a favor and gave him and his wife a baptism certificate. The elderly Nestrovsky wore it around his neck like a charm, but that did not give him any rest either. When the bandits would storm into town Nestrovsky and his wife were the first to run into the cellar and, lying in the dark corner with the baptism certificate around his neck, he quietly recited the viddui.

Aside from these two Jewish geniuses, there were no others in Dubova who were interested in seeking help from the good priest of Vilshanka. They only thought about fleeing, and the safe haven at that time was the lucky Jewish fortress of Holovanivsk, where a few hundred Jewish youth organized and armed themselves and would not allow any local or out-of-town bandits into the shtetl.

They used to tell tales of the miracles of these Holovanivsk youths. Legends about their heroism and exploits spread to every city and shtetl of the Kyiv region and Podilia, but there were very few lucky enough to get there, because on every road that led to Holovanivsk bandits ambushed Jews, whether in wagons or on foot. The bandits were dressed in various national colors. The colors depended on how far the Red armored car was from the Khrystynivka station. One could still occasionally find a Jewish wagon on the high road to Uman. But in Uman the authority used to change several times a day, just like the images change in a film. The Christian community from the four municipalities surrounding Uman would immediately accommodate to the authority of the moment, exchanging their red band for an inside-out jacket and right back again.

The Uman Jews were defenseless against every hue and color. In the city they were terrorized by the eighth so-called Soviet regiment who were merely an armed gang beneath a red flag. Decorated with red bands, they used to drive around the city and rob the Jewish population. They simply raped women in the streets, and at night they broke down the doors and windows of Jewish homes, demanding that they turn over their wives and daughters to them. Once they wanted to kill a Jewish girl because she captured men's hearts with her beauty.

These particular "Reds" were inside the city, and the national gangs were lurking outside the city, but they used to trade places with each other. So the city remained lawless, and then Kazimirik, the notorious leader of the Uman city thieves, was the only protector of the Jewish population. He had been in every jail, was a card player and a drunk. For many years his name was a defamatory word in Uman. In the gruesome summer days of the year 5679 he was the only one protecting the Uman Jews. Kazimirik sat on the roof of the Jewish hospital with his three Jewish friends, and with his machine gun sprayed fire and hailed bullets at the bandits, not allowing them into the city until the happy cannon shot of the Savior Angel, the Red armored car, was heard.

But at that time twenty Jewish families from Dubova did indeed flee to Uman, because after the "Red" regiment, there arrived in the city disciplined Soviet troops composed of Hungarians, Great-Russians, Chinese, and Jews. This group was protecting the Jewish population, and when they would leave a city, they happily took along Jews, women, and children, who, in fear of remaining without their protection, ran after them. One often met such military brigades of "Soviets" with wagons filled with Jewish women and children. They were often the last widows and orphans of a destroyed and killed-off Jewish community. The Dubova homeless in Uman, who fled because they could no longer bear the fear of death, also benefited from the hospitality of the Red army. It was also their fate after the "small" massacre in Dubova to survive the "quiet" massacre in Uman.

27

It was the 29th of June, on a sunny, fresh, early morning. The married and unmarried Polish women came out onto the Christian streets dressed in white, with flowers in their hands, to greet the united bandit groups of Sokol, Stetsiura, and Nikolsky,[57] who had entered Uman, with music and shouts of hoorah.

It turned out that afterwards, the Polish intelligentsia of Uman made excuses that they had been falsely informed about the arriving groups. Some suspicious people had told them that Polish military were marching into Uman. But the impact of the encounter was gruesome.

All three atamans came from the eminent Christian community of Uman. Two of them were the long-time Uman residents, Colonel Nikolsky, who already during the Russian tsarist period was an antisemite, and Sokol, his friend the Ukrainian public school teacher, who was a close relative of the famous priest Nikolsky of the Black Hundreds.[58] For the Uman Jews the fact that they were both connected to their Black Russian priest was significant. Prior to Kerensky the Jews with their kosher signatures freed the priest from the Kyiv jail, where he was under arrest and facing serious charges for inciting the people against the new regime.

The third ataman, Stetsiura, was the famous athlete giant of the Uman circus. He was the darling of the Uman public. His heroic appearance with his chestnut locks of hair won him many female admirers, Jewish girls among them. He gladly strolled with Jewish girls who were in love with him. But after the first massacre, when the Uman circus closed down, Stetsiura was left without any work, so he organized a gang out of the city's riffraff, and he went with them to rob and kill in the Jewish shtetls.

The "quiet" massacre in Uman lasted four hours. As soon as the bandits came in, it became frightfully quiet. In broad daylight, riding on a fine horse in the empty streets was the tall and robust Colonel Nikolsky in his white gloves, and at every moment his strong voice echoed through the sunny terrifying stillness, "Some more corpses, brothers! The more corpses the better!"

And again it was quiet ...

From time to time the choked voices of the tortured and raped cut through the air, and at the same time one heard the beautiful piano playing of the educated children in the Polish city-doctor's house ...

In the silence they were cutting off the limbs of fathers and mothers, sons and daughters, children and infants. And small Gentile girls watched with curiosity how they cut out the tongues of living people. Soldiers adorned with red silk piping went around to the Jewish houses looking for people, and Stetsiura, with his crew from the city, mainly raped women, and everywhere the families of his Jewish female admirers suffered.

And in this stillness five hundred school teachers from the community who were taking the provisional teacher-training courses in Ukrainian language, literature, and social sciences sent a delegation to the three ataman-bandits from Uman requesting support for their cultural establishment.

But there were a few righteous Christians in the city who were looking for ways to end the "quiet" bloodletting of the Jewish population. Because of this they invited Sokol to the municipal duma.

He made them wait for a long time for an answer, but he came to the meeting in the company of his two colleagues. The Christian representatives of the city in attendance greeted Sokol and his friends Stetsiura and Nikolsky. As Umaners they would certainly guard the peaceful residents of the city. To this Nikolsky answered that he was only a subordinate. He merely followed the orders of his ataman. And Sokol gave a clear answer, that, because the Jews of Krizhopil killed Ukrainian soldiers, the Jews of Uman were convicted by the authorities of national terrorism. Then a Christian representative, the Ukrainian teacher Khokhol, said that this innocent Jewish blood would be a sign of shame on the Ukrainian national movement, and then he loudly proclaimed that if what happened that morning had to happen again, they should kill him first.

This made an impression on Sokol, and he gave his word of honor that there would soon be order. And truly in the afternoon the bloodletting ceased. The Gentile women of the surrounding areas were still robbing the Jewish shops and carrying home the stolen goods, but the Christian intelligentsia did not show themselves in the streets.

28

After the "quiet" massacre in Uman a bit of good news reached Dubova, that in the city of Uman a way to reach the hearts of the Gentiles was already unfolding. The landowners, priests, students, teachers, nobility, everybody was allying with the Jews. The forlorn forsaken shtetl really liked this news, and the Dubova Jews also began to seek a way to reach the Gentile hearts in their community. Moyshe the wheelwright used all his influence as a proletarian who fed his wife and child by the labor of his own hands, and he managed to convince the "refined" Christians of the shtetl to put in a good word on behalf of the Dubova Jewish community. Just like the way they did in Uman, the Gentiles agreed that if a group of bandits stormed into shtetl, they would create a deputation of Jews and Christians who would beg for peace for the peaceful inhabitants.

Three Jews were appointed to the deputation. Aside from Moyshe the wheelwright and Gedalye Koretsky, the two elected community men, they also invited the lawyer Nestrovsky as another Jew, even though he had a conversion certificate written in black and white that he had already left the Jewish community. And willing to join in from the Christian side were the priest, the former Petliura officer Andrei Ovtsharuk (out of gratitude because the Dubova Jews begged for his life from the Red Russian bastards from Novoarkhangelsk), the free-thinker and Jewish-friendly Dimitri Shabolinski, and Kopnik and Smelnitski, the two advocates hired by the Jewish community.

And they did not have to wait long for their chance. The Red armored car had allowed Sokol to leave Uman, so Sokol then went to Holovanivsk to take revenge on their Jewish self-defense group. Dubova was along the way, so twenty-five of his horsemen split off and went into the shtetl to play a game with the Dubova Jews.

It was Friday during the day. Hearing the sounds of hoorah and whistling, the shtetl Jews immediately ran into the orchards. The loyal Jewish soldier Moyshe the wheelwright, who remained at his post, immediately ran to gather the deputation together, but when he arrived at Gedalye Koretsky's he found that Gedalye had already hidden himself somewhere. The lawyer Nestrovsky agreed to go with Moyshe, but upon nearing the place where the bandits were located, he, with his conversion certificate around his neck, suddenly disappeared somewhere. Moyshe went by himself to the bridge to call together the appointed Christians. A group of local Gentiles was standing near the militia administration. So Moyshe began to ask that one of them take him to the priest, as the priest had promised that he would be in the deputation. But nobody wanted to go with him. Everybody advised Moyshe that he should not look for deputation members, and that he himself should hide, because here in Dubova they were going to do exactly what they did in Uman. Dimitri Shabolinski, who was standing by the door of his house, told him the same thing.

In the end Dorotei, the old barber, who actually had two sons who were bandits, called out that he would go with Moyshe to the priest. But at that moment two bandit horsemen jumped down with guns in hand pointed directly at Moyshe. Smelnitski, the leader of the militia, quickly called Moyshe into the courtyard. The horsemen became angry and began to yell, "What kind of dirty Jew are they hiding in the militia courtyard?" But Smelnitski answered them firmly, "the Jew is ours and no outsiders are allowed to interfere here." The rest of the peasant group was silent. Afterward Smelnitski added that the Jew had to collect the 30,000 ruble contribution that they were demanding. Also, that he would be getting them food and boots.

The bandits gave them an hour's time to do this, and if everything were not ready by that minute they would take the dark-haired Jew with them.

After these clear words Moyshe the wheelwright ran into the orchards looking for the hidden Jewish householders for them to give him money, and in this way he collected the 30,000 rubles. Meanwhile the militia leader Smelnitski provided vodka and food for the twenty-five horsemen at the expense of the Jewish community. But in Dubova ten pairs of boots were not available. Moyshe the wheelwright and Smelnitski had to beg them to forgo this, as there was no place to buy them. They did. Taking the money, they left the shtetl calmly.

It was already evening.

Moyshe again ran into the orchards with the good news. Among the blooming fields and gardens he called out in a loud voice that the Jews should go to the synagogue and the women should hurry home to bless the Shabbos candles.

29

After the miracle with Sokol's bandit horsemen, the Dubova Jews again began to think about how to protect their lives. There was now nothing to hope for from the awakened feelings of pity in the Gentiles' hearts. The shtetl's bandit fund was also getting smaller and smaller. Whoever still had a little bit of money and jewelry was afraid to let it out of their hands, so that at the last minute they would have something with which to bribe their way out of death. In order to cover the community bandit expenses they even wanted to sell the Gentiles two large opulent Jewish homes owned by rich and fortunate landowners who had been lucky enough to sneak into the protected Holovanivsk while there was still time. Though the Uman area was then under the authority of Kozakov and his army of robbers, in the moment of danger, when the Red armored car arrived in Uman with its cannon thunder, Dubova was cut off from Uman by the local Dubova peasant population who would hide Kozakov and his bandits, because he, Kozakov, had distributed Jewish property and goods to them.

In the shtetl everyone was waiting in fear for "news." Every day there were small groups of people standing around in the streets. Everyone was idle. Young and old yearned to hear what was being said, and the rumors were driving people crazy. Aside from the hunchback female telephone operator, who would provide news about Kozakov, that he was going to slaughter everyone from the elderly down to infants in Dubova, a local peasant youth who had been with the bandit gang of the three atamans near Holovanivsk also brought a greeting from Kozakov. He was an experienced "soldier" in Petliura's army, who came from the front wearing expensive rings and used to boast that Proskuriv and Teplik happened to kill fourteen Jews on his watch. He also delivered the news that Kozakov was still going to come to Dubova.

The Dubova Jews again started to safeguard their lives and their remaining belongings. In great secrecy from their Gentile neighbors, they built "hiding places" in the depths of the earth, dug holes and recesses in the walls of their cellars, and blocked their attics with bricks and stones, leaving cleverly hidden openings to crawl into. Afterward they sat by their locked doors and gates and listened to every sound. In the quiet one could hear their hearts beating. The shtetl clocks broke the dead silence, counting the hours in the endless interval waiting for something dreadful. In the meantime, the Jewish dead were brought into the shtetl from all directions, and one had to attend to the burials on a daily basis.

But still hope lived on, a ray of light shined over the forsaken community of Jews that was sentenced to death. Someone who fled from Uman said that America had sent an army to save the Jews of Ukraine. With the help of the American army, American Jews were going to save their old mothers and fathers, brothers and sisters, wives, and children.

Until Tisha b'Av[59] the people in Dubova were comforted by this sweet bright hope.

30

The Petliura "soldier" spoke truth. Kozakov really did come to Dubova. Tuesday was Tisha b'Av, and on Wednesday morning three thousand men from his bandit army came into the shtetl with music, Ukrainian folk songs, and drunken cries of hoorah.

The arrival of that particular unit captured the eye with a color display of all sorts of hues. Among the many red flags embroidered with gold and heavy braided trimming also fluttered a Ukrainian yellow-blue flag of soft expensive silk edged in velvet fringe, hanging on a silver pole. Kozakov himself dazzled with the gleam of his clothes. Instead of the intellectual-democratic French coat and jodhpurs, he wore red baggy trousers with an embroidered black velvet waistcoat. A golden watch chain was hanging on his chest, and his hands were striped with expensive bracelets and rings.

The thirty men from his mobile headquarters were also dressed in the same way. The "soldiers" were wearing embroidered shirts with red belts and tasseled bands on their hats. This time they were composed exclusively of peasant youth from the villages and rabble from the Christian cities. One could barely see a cultured face in the crowd. But there were a few students among the bandits, and later the priest even justified them, saying that Satan had enticed them to rape Jewish women and that their hands were clean of blood.

Among the six horsemen who came along as spectators there was even a student. Immediately the Dubova Jews fled into the peasant orchards and gardens, and the lucky ones that had established "secret" places at home hid themselves.

Meanwhile Moyshe the wheelwright grabbed an old Jew in the street and went with him to call on Kopnik and Smelnitski, the Jewish community's hired protectors.

When all four of them arrived at the telephone station where the spectators had stopped to speak on the telephone, all six of them were standing outside the door. Smelnitski introduced the Jewish delegates to them. Sitting on their horses, they glanced at the two Jews and ordered them to feed and reshoe the horses, and said that they themselves were also hungry. Moyshe immediately sent a smith for the horses, and he invited all six horsemen to his house to eat something. Along with them came the two Gentile defenders of the community. Moyshe's wife set the table. Immediately they brought out vodka, bread, sausages, and herring, and Moyshe himself became more resolute. He sat comfortably among the "guests" to tell them a few words of truth, that he, as a Jewish proletarian, would propose to their ataman that he call together the local businessmen of Dubova for them to point out which Jews in the shtetl were communists.

One of the six outsiders who was sitting at the table answered him that they, the loyal soldiers of Ataman Kozakov, would forgo asking the locals who was guilty. "Now is the time that we have to kill all the Zhids, and immediately!"

The Jew that Moyshe grabbed in the street as delegate stood at the side in deathly fear, and a few other Jews with their eyes rolling in fear quietly came to ask what was happening. Moyshe answered them that everyone should just do what they thought, and he himself called Kopnik away from the table and asked him to discuss with the bandits whether perhaps they wanted money.

Meanwhile the "guests" realized that they were sitting in a Jewish house, and they immediately got up to leave. In the meantime, they sent Moyshe for cigarettes, and they got angry at the unlucky petrified delegate and ordered him to get out of their sight right away.

When Moyshe brought the cigarettes, all six horsemen were already sitting in the militia administration around a flask of vodka. Kopnik came out of there to meet Moyshe with a clear answer: that they wanted a "tribute" of 200,000 rubles in Ukrainian money. Then Moyshe begged him to try to bargain, because in the shtetl there remained only a few groshen. Because of this situation Moyshe pleaded with the peasants standing there to put in a good word. But Kopnik came right back out and reported that they didn't want to take the 200,000 anymore, because they said that in any case they would kill everybody and everything would end up being theirs. Nevertheless, Kopnik said to him, "Come, Moyshe, let's go to Kozakov ourselves."

But Moyshe was too shaken up and devastated, so he answered him that he couldn't go. Kopnik should go with Smelnitski, and he would wait where he was. He would immediately take it upon himself to arrange whatever was needed. Then, in a desperate state, he again pleaded with the surrounding peasants to do something so an entire town of innocent people would not be slaughtered. But the group was silent ... Kopnik and Smelnitski each left separately, but immediately they had to run back. Shots were heard from the village. The bandit army was already at the bridge. They stormed into the shtetl with a fanfare, with swords gleaming against the sun and flags held high.

"You are all doomed!" Kopnik shook his head at the forlorn Moyshe the wheelwright. "They are already killing ..."

It was at the bridge that the first Jewish victim was struck down. It was Isak Vinitsky, the lawyer Nestrovsky's son-in-law. His personal friend was Andrei Ovtsharuk, the Ukrainian Petliura-intellectual who was sitting with a book throughout this. They used to socialize for hours and read together. That morning they were both sitting under a tree in Ovtsharuk's garden reading newspapers that Vinitsky fortuitously got somewhere. Upon seeing the bandits, Andriusha ran into the house, and Vinitsky ran after him, but when Isak had his foot on the doorstep, Andriusha blocked the door, and they shot him under his window.

Meanwhile Moyshe ran to his own home, and for the first time he led his wife and their five children down into the cellar. The mother had already sent the other two children to Berislavsky the furrier's "secret hiding place." They were a girl of fourteen and a small boy of six. The small boy cried a lot and didn't want to leave his mother, but she was afraid that she had too many children with her, so by force she sent the boy and girl away.

Moyshe had secured his six souls well and along with them two sisters who were his neighbors, young wives with tiny children in their arms. He hid them in the cellar among the rims which he used to make the wheels. He also blocked the door with wood from his workshop. He supplied them with bread and lowered a bucket of sour cherries into the cellar. Then Moyshe himself fled to the smiths' street, where the Jewish smiths looked at him confused and lost ... they were standing by the open doors wringing their hands and they stuttered in fear, "If Moyshe is running away it is already bad ...."

He ran past them and dashed into the workshop of a Gentile smith. There he threw down his jacket and began to work. They heard from across the street the hoarse and choked-up voices of two Jews who were dragged out of a Gentile yard to be beat up. Moyshe banged his own fingers with a hammer, and his eyes went blood-red. He asked the smith's son for a favor, that he go to Kopnik and let him know where he, Moyshe, was. If they needed him, he was ready.

Meanwhile the old smith told him to leave. No matter how much Moyshe begged him, the smith had only one thing in mind, he was afraid of revenge. They were saying that no decent person was allowed to hide a Jew. Even so, he had pity on Moyshe and showed him a shed near the smithy with an attic where he could hide himself. Moyshe went into the hiding place, and there he was waiting for news from the young smith. This is how the day passed. The heat was great, and in the surrounding sunny golden fields they were cutting the ripe grain, and along with this, the screaming of those being raped and tortured to death split the bright blue skies.

In the evening the smith came. He tossed up the jacket and hat that Moyshe had left in the workshop, and then he himself went up into the attic to tell Moyshe what was happening in the shtetl.

The news was brief. Kopnik and Smelnitski said they couldn't do anything. Then he recited the names of twenty-four people that he saw lying dead in the street. Also he heard in the village that the "soldiers" were going to stay the whole night. It was very joyous in the village, guitars and harmonicas were playing, there was drinking in the yards at set tables, the young were dancing, and all the girls were giving the "soldiers" rings and bracelets.

Moyshe spent the night in the attic in pain and anger, listening to the lamenting and suffering cries of the people dying.

In the morning someone began to ring the bells loudly in the churches as if there were a fire. Moyshe immediately sent the young smith for news. He soon came back and reported to him that the ataman was calling the local peasants to a meeting. Then Moyshe sent him to Kopnik with a request, that he and Smelnitski should both persuade the decent householders of the Dubova village to beg the ataman to stop the bloodletting on their behalf. He also asked the smith to go to Moyshe's cellar to find out about his family, let them know that he was alive, and to throw some pieces of bread down to the children.

In a few hours the smith came with news. Ataman Kozakov called together the village near the church and told them that the time had now come to kill all the Jews, and asked if they would agree to this. And the householders of the village answered that he was allowed to do whatever he wanted with the Jews, but he should not touch the Jewish smiths, because it was harvest time so they couldn't manage without them. The ataman said, "Fine." He would allow the smiths to live. The smith also reported to Moyshe that his entire family in the cellar was alive. "Soldiers" went there a few times, but the children were sleeping and it was quiet, so they went away. Then he threw down a piece of bread for the children.

Moyshe lived with this bit of news until afternoon, when the smith brought him his son Khananye, crying and confused, from the cellar. Khananye told Moyshe that everybody had to flee from the cellar because it was Thursday, and so as usual the peasants rode into the market, and all day long they were robbing Jewish houses and stores and packing the goods into their wagons for themselves. The bandits were killing and dragging everything away with them. They also invaded the wheel warehouse and in so doing they uncovered the hiding place. Immediately the bandits came running and told everybody to get out. They chased the two women with the small children in their arms somewhere, and he, Khananye, pleaded with them for his life and that of his mother and the children. He told them that his father was a poor worker and that he didn't know where he was. After this the mother and children ran to Kopnik, and Khananye himself left to look for his father.

Moyshe and Khananye passed the day in the attic, listening to the noise from the shtetl market along with the cries of fear of those being tortured to death. In the evening the smith brought them a bit of news, that the ataman ordered the people in the market to take all the Jewish corpses and throw them into the lime pits at the base of the mountain where they discarded the carcasses of horses and cattle.

Moyshe heard this and immediately got to work. He told Khananye to write a letter to the priest, which he would dictate to him word for word, that he, the priest, should call together honorable people and beg them to at least save the women and children. And the smith was to carry the letter to him.

The smith took the letter and got down from the attic, but immediately he turned back with the piece of paper in hand and with strong words he ordered, "Moshke, get yourself out of here!" Meanwhile he consoled Moyshe that Petliura's Ataman Pavlov came into Uman and gave Kozakov an order to stop killing women and children, but the "soldiers" would again remain overnight in Dubova.

Moyshe and Khananye began to beg the smith to let them stay in the attic for the night, but he, the Gentile, did not let himself be persuaded, and he threatened them that he would reveal their hiding place to his mother-in-law who was notorious as a robber many years ago.

"Come my child," Moyshe said to Khananye, "Let us go home to die ..."

They kissed each other and went down from the attic into the smith's orchard, where beyond its fence the wet lime pits were located. They agreed to go separately, so that maybe one of them would survive, and they once again embraced and kissed, but in that instant, they heard the hysterical cries of the old Khaye Shkodnik, whom local bandits were dragging alive into her grave.

Khananye tore himself away from his father's arms and ran somewhere into the field, and Moyshe himself quietly sneaked through the hedges like a cat to his own cellar, and there he immediately fell into a faint ...

When he woke up it was already midday. Once again, as if there were a fire, they were ringing the church bells. Moyshe heard the local Gentiles in the storeroom above him take his wheel rims, and someone was deliberating about whether one was allowed to take from strangers, and various voices answered from all sides, "It is already ours regardless. They've killed everybody." Moyshe also heard that they were ringing the church bells to call a meeting, that they wanted to ask the ataman to take pity on the women and children.

Moyshe was lying in the cellar on the cold earth and he looked blankly into the darkness. His brow was wet from a cold sweat, and he was completely numb. Somewhere music was playing. Soldiers were singing songs, and upstairs in the storeroom, familiar voices were calling out his name. It was Kopnik and Smelnitski coming to see how he was doing and they went looking for him in the cellar.

"Come out Moshke!" they called out, "They are going away already."

But Moyshe could not move himself from the spot. So they went down and led him out by the hand. Local Gentiles were still standing around, so they handed him a drink of water and gave him the news that his wife and children were alive and that they had hidden Khananye in a field. Moyshe took off his hat with the crest and along with everyone else he set about gathering the sheaves.

"Are there any Jews remaining in the town?" Moyshe asked them.

"Few ..."

"Where are the women and children?"

"At Dimitri Shabolinski's. He turned his house into a shelter and took everybody in."

"And where are the dead?"

"In the lime pits. But now it is already quiet." They calmed him down. "They just killed the rabbi's son, and that's it ...."

Moyshe grasped his head in both hands and with wild cries ran into the street.

31

And again, miracles happened.

During the great massacre in Dubova the entire Jewish community perished, and nevertheless one saw the miracles of God. Miraculously a few widows and orphans survived and this miracle occurred because of a small child.

Thursday during the day, when they uncovered the hiding place of his family at Moyshe the wheelwright's house, the two women who were not his relatives ran into the street carrying their tiny children in their arms. One of them slipped into a Gypsy's house and survived, and the other one ran to the smiths, where many people were hiding because the bandits circumvented their houses and workshops in accord with the request of the local peasants. But it was very crowded and hot in the smithy and so the woman ran to her house, but while she was running across the street a bandit caught her and wanted to rape her. It was the tall and robust Sarah Nimerovsky. So she fought back until that man split her head with a sword.

She fell. Her fresh blood sprayed on the child, and the child began to scream. Then the bandit took the child in his arms and started to quiet him down, but the child was still screaming. This annoyed him. Even though he immediately had pity on it, the cries of the small creature exasperated him. So he took him in his arms still screaming and carried it to the lime pits, but Gentile women were standing there, curiously looking at how they were throwing dead and living people into the wet graves. They then said, it is a great sin before God to throw such a small innocent creature into the grave alive, and one of these Gentile women took the child from the arms of the murderer and carried it to the Christian cooperative. There, a large peasant group, mostly women, surrounded the child, and one of them, a young one, with her own small child in her arms called out that she would nurse the Jewish infant and would take it home.

But in the blue of dawn the Gentile woman brought the screaming child back to the cooperative. In no way did the child want to take the unfamiliar breast of the young nursing mother. This made a great impression on the surrounding peasant women, and they began to scream that it was an abomination to kill mothers of small children. God will not forgive anyone for it. Then the "free thinking" Dimitri Shabolinski intervened and presented a plan, that he would order the ringing of the church bells for all the householders of the village to gather for a meeting, and that they, the Gentile women, should demand at the meeting that the ataman order his men not to kill any more women or children. He, Dimitri, was giving them his home as a shelter, saying that they should all be brought to him.

It was already Friday morning on the third day of the massacre, when only 110 widows and about two hundred orphans remained in the shtetl.

32

On the same morning another miracle happened. It happened in the rabbi's home.

In truth, nothing new happened there. During the first massacre the local inside-out-jacket wearers spared his home, and on the 20th of Sivan the out-of-town bandits did not even touch so much as a necklace there either.

These facts made a great impression on the shtetl, and they began to believe that in Dubova the bandits had no power over the rabbi's home, so every single person that had anything expensive to hide came to the rebbetzin with a request that she herself put it away and that it be in the area where the rabbi was situated.

All the rebbetzin's drawers and chests were filled with strangers' possessions. They brought her jewelry, packets of all types of currency whose names she didn't even know. They hung expensive fur coats and silk clothes in her every corner, truly they brought a fortune to her.

Whenever a gang would storm in, young and old would run to the rabbi's house. Whoever managed to fit inside was certain that they would remain alive because of the rabbi's virtue. The rebbetzin had flour, and so she baked cakes and fed the people until—with God's help—the danger was over.

In such days of unrest, the old rabbi steeled himself to get dressed, and he was always lying on the couch in the study with an open holy book on the table next to him. From time to time, he would call the rebbetzin and tell her to make sure to give tea to those breastfeeding the small children. He often called his son to switch his book for him. But he ate very little and basically lived on medicinal drops that refreshed and strengthened his heart.

This is what it was like the entire summer until Tisha b'Av, until the great massacre.

On the day after Tisha b'Av, when the bandit army tore into Dubova with their gleaming knives and swords raised high, the shtetl as usual ran to the rabbi's home, where the killers did not have any power.

As she always did, the rebbetzin began to bake cake, and the samovar on the table was soon boiling for the nursing women and the small children. The rabbi himself asked his son to dress him: he wanted to lie in his study on the couch. At every moment Jews, women and children, scared to death, ran in from the street. The home became very crowded. Every room, the kitchen, the entryway, everywhere was full of people. All the Dubova Jews wanted to save their lives through the protection of their sick old rabbi.

This lasted a few hours; afterward a tragedy occurred.

Suddenly there was a bang on the wall, the clang of shattering window panes, and a few young bandits tore into the rabbi's home with swords and ramrods in their hands. Immediately they hurled themselves at the rabbi who was quietly lying on the made-up couch. They hurled themselves at him with wild cries, and they laid their impure hands onto the bones of the emaciated old man.

A dull yammering cry tore out through the open door into the street, and in horror and fear the community ran from the rabbi's home to wherever their eyes would lead them.

Thus fell the last fortress the Dubova Jews had.

The bandits beat the rabbi fiercely. Blood poured out of his ears. They twisted one of his arms behind him, but aside from him they didn't touch anybody else. They immediately threw themselves at the drawers and chests, where the little bit of remaining wealth of the shtetl was lying hidden. It dazzled their eyes.

The bandits were so bewitched by the money and jewelry that they forgot about the people. But all these valuable items that the Dubova householders and housewives had turned over to the care of the rebbetzin created a nest of hidden riches in the rabbi's home at a time when all the Jewish houses of the shtetl were already empty.

The first few bandit-soldiers, who by chance tore in there, came out laden with money and jewelry, and this was related from one bandit to the other. In this way a rumor spread among them that there was a hidden treasure in the zhid rabbi's home, and so everybody went there to get packets of all types of currency and gold and silver objects.

They tore in each time in groups with axes and cudgels, searching through drawers and chests and all sorts of household items, breaking everything that came into their hands.

The rabbi was lying in his study on the couch, which was piled high with layers of bedding, and near him on the table the book was still lying open. The rebbetzin was sitting quietly near him on a chair and she was putting cold compresses on his head. The bandits went wild, they broke tables and chairs, overturned the emptied cupboards, smashed up the oven, but they did not glance at them, the two old people, as if they weren't right there in front of them.

But this all happened until there was nothing left to take in the house. At the end the gold ten-pieces along with the jewelry of the Dubova Jews ran out, and then the bandits glanced at the silent old couple in the smashed-up and picked-through study.

Upon finding the overturned cupboards to be empty, the bandits started attacking the sickly old rabbi with cudgels.

"Tell us old devil, where did you hide the money?" they kept yelling at him, hitting him with the stocks of their rifles.

The Dubova rabbi continued to lie quietly on the couch with the neatly arranged pillows flecked with his freshly spilled blood and with the open book on the table near him, and the determined rebbetzin was pleading. She swore that she had no more money. This particular stubbornness of the old couple, who did not want to tell the secret of where they had hidden their fortune, enraged the bandits.

And they turned to torture, intending in that way to extract the truth, and they only tortured the rabbi. They started pouring buckets of water on him from the full barrel that was standing in the kitchen. Then they dragged him down to the floor and kicked him in the head. When they left, the rebbetzin put a pillow down on the floor under his head. He asked her to prop the open book on a chair for him.

This particular scene, of a wounded bloody old man lying on the floor with the open book next to him brought forth wild laughter from the bandits. As a group they continued together searching for gold and packs of Tsar Nikolai banknotes.

"Speak, old devil, where is the zhid god?" they cried out with wild laughter jabbing him with their swords.

The Dubova rabbi in the end responded, saying to the rebbetzin, "Tell them in their language, 'It is better if they shoot me.'"

"Better if you shoot him!" she repeated word for word in Ukrainian.

Wild laughter interrupted her words, which she uttered while sobbing with tears of grief. "Speak, where is the zhid god?"

"Master of the Universe, I accept the suffering. I receive it with love ... but I cannot bear the desecration of G-d's name ... ask them once more ... ask in their language ....a bullet .... I cannot bear the desecration of G-d's name ... in their language ..."

He spoke feebly with half words, but the rebbetzin repeated what he said tenderly and sincerely after him in Ukrainian, begging and crying. She also begged for a bullet for herself ....

But Kozakov's bandits did not shoot the Dubova rabbi and rebbetzin. They tortured him from Wednesday to Friday morning, and the rebbetzin was standing watch, taking care of his kosher soul. Throughout this she thought that he was dying, even though he was speaking and still making sense. But he recited the viddui, and his voice became more far off and feeble.

The rebbetzin dressed him in white clothes. The tallis and the shroud for the dead were also ready lying above, because she intended to be ready for the minute that his kosher soul left, and then she would run somewhere to find two or three older Jews who could immediately bring him to burial, so that the killers would at least not defile his corpse.

This is what the rebbetzin was thinking, but she also had another plan. A thought came to her to muster up her strength and carry him somewhere, not too far, into a Gentile's garden. There they would stop beating him, and maybe he would survive. But she could not move from the spot, because while sitting in the house she was guarding the attic where her son and daughter-in-law and children were lying hidden.

That son was Mendl, the youngest brother of Mikha Yoysef Berditshevsky.

This particular son, born to the Dubova rabbi in his old age, was someone punished by God. He was already an adult of thirty-seven years, a father of six children. His oldest son had already served in the army, and he remained as handsome as when he was a groom, as if he were just coming out from under the chuppah.[60] His beautiful black eyes in which the fire of youth still flickered and his dark head of curly hair along with his height and straight posture drew suspicion. Mendl Berditshevsky looked like a communist, and because of this in the summer of 5679 the fear was greater for him than for all of the other young people of Dubova. As soon as there was unrest in the town, they had to hide Mendl the rabbi's son first so that he and his beautiful black locks would not be conspicuous.

His place was always in his father's attic.

On the first day of the great massacre, when the bandits took control of the rabbi's house, his wife and their five small children, and a Jewish butcher, the rabbi's neighbor, also went up to the attic to Mendl.

There they settled themselves quite comfortably, with blankets, a pail of water, a tin of sugar, and bread and butter. Afterward they took away the ladder, and the old couple remained below so that nobody would realize that there was anyone else in the home aside from them.

But afterward there was a misfortune. Reyzele, Mendl's seven-year-old daughter, would under no circumstances sit in the attic with her father and mother. She would rather be with Zeyde and Bobe down below. Out of fear that she would cry, they complied with Reyzele and let her down below. The girl was with the old couple the entire time. When the bandits tore in to beat her Zeyde, Reyzele hid herself under the oven, and nobody could see her. Afterward she would sit on the floor with her Bobe and watch how she put compresses on her Zeyde's head.

Until Thursday night this was how Reyzele remained down below with her Bobe and Zeyde.

But late after midnight the child suddenly began to be afraid of the bandits. She begged to be with her mother, and as the old woman settled her back into the attic, she cried to her mother, "Mother, I am afraid ... the bandits have poked out Zeyde's eyes ..."

It was already dawn. The rabbi was already lying like someone who was dead, but he still spoke a few words. He was still begging for a bullet, "In their language ... beg ... in their language ... Esther ...."

But the rebbetzin was not listening to him then. At the last minute she had to forsake her trusted post. She was sitting on the stoop with a split open head, bathed in her own blood, and with all her strength she was beating her chest saying, *al chet*.[61] She had already said the viddui to herself, but meanwhile she begged and pleaded, just like out of a *tkhine*,[62] for God to watch over her nest with the small birds in the attic. She begged on behalf of the small children.

But in that minute once again a gang of young bandits ran in. A Gentile woman who happened to be passing by with a pitcher of water in hand tore her, the fainting rebbetzin, from the bandits' hands. The bandits were ready to leave, but in that moment someone coughed in the attic.

It was the rabbi's neighbor, Moyshe the butcher, who all his life was a cougher. For three days the rabbi's daughter-in-law fed him sugar so he wouldn't cough, but nonetheless in the end he coughed.

There was joy among the bandits. With wild cries and laughter, they dragged everyone down from the attic, and naturally as soon as they saw Mendl they began to yell, "Communist!"

The local Gentiles immediately undressed him and measured his clothes against themselves. Mendl Berditshevsky was always dressed in the nicest and the best. There was a big fight among the Gentiles over his beautiful shirt, and they could not decide who would get the shoes. One shoe ended up with one Gentile, and the other—with another.

Afterward they killed Mendl. And because they saw with their own eyes that he was truly a communist, they chopped off all his fingers and toes. The simple Jew, Moyshe the butcher, was simply shot.

And then the miracle happened.

Exactly at that moment they started ringing the church bells. It was already Friday morning. Well before sunrise they had called a meeting. The Dubova Gentiles were already tired of dragging the Jewish dead to their graves, so on the third day of the massacre they demanded of Kozakov that they stop killing women and children. That was how the old rebbetzin with the split-open head and her young daughter-in-law Yente Berditshevsky with her five small children survived. They took them to shelter at Dimitri Shabolinski's, so that he, the good Gentile, would watch over them.

And the church bells were still ringing. The sun rose and the Gentiles were still gathering up the dead. A large wagon with a pair of robust horses rode over to the rabbi's house. It was full to the brim with murdered Jewish men, women and children, and the two Gentiles threw Moyshe the butcher and the rabbi and his son up onto that mountain of corpses, the two of them sharing the tallis and shroud that the rebbetzin had kept at the ready.

They drove the rabbi to the base of the mountain and threw him down into the lime pits along with his entire community of Jews.

33

And yet another miracle happened during these days of massacre in Dubova.

Wednesday evening when pigs and dogs were already dragging torn-off human limbs around in the streets, sixty-three young men and women from Dubova, who had been working in the beet fields near the sugar factory of the village of Peregonovka, came into town. They were the children of Jewish householders, who at that time had been seeking the opportunity to hire themselves out for physical labor in the peasant community of the villages, so that in the eyes of the local Gentiles they would not appear as idlers. These particular youth workers came home on Shabbos Nachamu,[63] tanned and strong from air and sunshine, after working for six weeks in the fields.

But they were greeted by the young people of the Dubova village streets with cries of hoorah, mocking laughter, and stone throwing. The sixty-three teenagers took off over the bridge into the shtetl right into the hands of the bandits.

But God performed a miracle. A door opened from a peasant's garden far down the riverbank, and an old peasant quietly let everyone into his orchard. It was the yard of the two brothers Anton and Reyer Melnik. They kept the Jewish boys and girls hidden in their garden for three days, cooked potatoes for them, and gave them bread and water. And Friday afternoon after the bandits left, both good Gentiles let them out of their hiding place for them to go look for their fathers and mothers. But almost all of their families had been murdered and thrown into the lime pits.

34

But the greatest miracle happened with the Dubova smiths.

They were three Jewish families and out of the entire Jewish community only they were granted the right to survive because their labor was needed at the peasant farms. In truth the ataman bandit Kozakov happily gave them this particular privilege because they, the Jewish smiths of Dubova, were also greatly needed by him. During all three bright summer days of the great massacre, they shoed the horses of the bandit army and sharpened their swords to destroy the Jewish shtetl, and they were the only living Jewish witnesses of the humiliating and violent deaths that these impure Gentile minds devised to torture their Jewish victims.

The Jewish smiths saw how they dragged alive into the grave Khaye Shkodnik, the grandmother of the converted Feyge-Vitele. Her screams pierced their ears. So they shot her, and then she finally kept quiet. But when they threw her into the lime pit among young men and Jews with beards, she completely covered up her legs with her dress ...

And the local bandits forced Shmuel-Yitskhok to die such a humiliating death that the entire market was doubled over with laughter. He, the arrogant one who during every misfortune of the shtetl sat by himself in his beautiful opulent house, was overtaken by fear on the second day of the great massacre. He and Khaye ran to a poor honest peasant in the village, someone with whom he had dealt for years and for whom he did great favors, taking along their money with the gold and silver. At that moment when he was afraid of death, it seemed to him that the best Gentile in Dubova was the poor and honest Onisko Tshernovol, and as soon as he handed over his fortune to him, he turned him over to the bandits. But Shmuel kept the green thousands for himself. He wanted to buy himself out of being killed with the money, but instead the local Gentiles whispered to the bandits that he, Shmuel-Yitskhok, loved his money very much, and so the bandits forced him to dance across the street with his green thousands in his hands to his wet grave-for-the-living.

The Dubova smiths also saw how the bandit soldiers carried the beautiful and young daughter-in-law of Yoysef Solodovnik on a spike. She was a great beauty and was nineteen years old. She was born and raised in Holovanivsk by impoverished parents, and at age sixteen she completed the Gymnasium, and at eighteen she became a pharmacist. Half a year earlier she married Zalmen Solodovnik out of love, and they were a couple happily in love.

On the first day of the massacre they killed Zalmen before her very eyes. Afterward the bandits turned to her. They were reflecting on her beauty, and thereupon they tore off her clothes, yanking her from each other's hands. But she calmed them all down. She smiled at them and tenderly caressed their heads. She called them all into her husband's perfume shop, where she would give everybody nice-smelling soaps, and she would pour eau du cologne on herself, and then she would go with them into her "bedroom."

The bandits allowed themselves to be persuaded and went off with her to her husband's perfume shop, and there before everybody's eyes she poisoned herself with carbolic acid. The young bandits were as angry as wolves, and they carried her out into the street on a spike, but she was already dead.

The smiths were also silent witnesses of the martyr's death of the seventy-year-old Gemara teacher Pesach Zborsky of Dubova.

During the days of the massacres in the summer of 5679 he, the great scholar and quiet, pious Jew, was always sitting at home over a holy book. His elderly wife with their children and grandchildren were hidden in the attic, and he quietly watched over their home, but he began to recite Psalms loudly when he would hear the screams of those being tortured to death.

And God had always favored him, nobody paid attention to his small crooked home. But in the great massacre his poor quiet nest was also robbed. It was after the first day, and in the morning at market time an angry drunken band stormed into his house again. They immediately discovered the hiding place in the attic. They dragged everyone down. Before his very eyes they killed his children and grandchildren, and he continued to recite Psalms loudly. Then they dragged him alone into the street, where the market was teeming. They first chopped off the hand in which he was holding the book of Psalms. The book fell to the ground, but the Jewish man bent down and picked it up with his other hand. They then chopped off his other hand, and the old Gemara teacher still did not cease reciting the verses loudly. So throughout the ringing cadences of his Psalm declamations they chopped limbs from him until he was silent. Then the murderers forced his blind old wife to wash her husband's blood from the swords, and then they killed her with the same cold steel.

A lucky son of the smith families of Dubova also witnessed the last minutes of the Zionist intellectual and community activist Gedalye Koretsky.

When the bandits attacked his beautiful middle-aged wife to rape her in their home, he ran out onto the porch and he began to yell in Russian, "I am a communist, long live Lenin and Trotsky!" Then he began to sing the Marseillaise and, while singing, he fell dead next to his raped wife, shot in the head and with his arms and legs broken in half.

Passing by the open doors of the Jewish-owned smithies, the bandits also dragged the metal worker from Ladyzhynka along with his twelve-year-old only son into their lime-pit graves alive. They were grabbed in the street while they were holding hands, wounded and faint, asking for a bit of water from the local Gentiles.

They also decapitated the young pregnant wife Esther Dinshteyn before the very eyes of the smiths. In the middle of the street her black combed head with the barrettes below her ears was lying in the dust and dirt, and next to it was the fetus that they had removed from her cut-open belly, which the bandits had been throwing around just like a toy balloon.

The smiths' ears also heard the mocking laughter of the local Gentiles, when the wagoner Shloyme Teplitsky demanded that the bandits shoot him, and as they were hacking him with their swords, the surrounding peasant group doubled over with laughter, bantering with each other as to why he wasn't letting himself be cut.

Also, as the bandits were taking Shoyl Nakhimovitsh to the wet lime pits, the Jewish smiths did him a favor. There with his three-year-old son, he asked the smiths for the favor of sharpening the sword well, and the bandits agreed to it. One of the smiths sharpened it, and the bandits made Shoyl's head fly all the way to the forges, splattering the walls with a rain of blood, and they hurled the three-year-old child alive down into the Jewish community grave.

And the Dubova smiths saw the mocking death of the elderly lawyer Nestrovsky and his wife, whom they dragged out of a grain elevator paralyzed with fear, him with his conversion certificate around his neck. He showed the bandits the amulet that the Vilshanka priest put on him. They tore it up in the midst of applause and screams of hoorah from the local Gentiles. And nobody knew how the Nestrovsky couple perished, because they were both killed with such a disgraceful, humiliating death that it cannot be recounted with any human language ...

With this ended the testimony of the Dubova smiths about the great massacre of the 10th, 11th, and the morning of the 12th of the month of Av,[64] 5679, and in addition we have received another precise chronicle from Moyshe the wheelwright, the Dubova proletarian member of the Jewish community council, who was standing watch in the destroyed Jewish shtetl until its end.

35

On Friday morning, when Moyshe the wheelwright came out of the cellar, he immediately had to serve at his community post.

After he ran into the street shouting wildly and stumbled upon the local peasant youth near the rabbi's house fighting over the shoes and the jacket of Mendl Berditshevsky, Dimitri Shabolinski came up to him with a question, "What should we do? The women and children are hungry."

This was well before noon when a few bandit soldiers were still wandering around the shtetl.

In this same Dimitri's house, Kozakov and his staff were still having breakfast at tables set in white with music playing. During all three days of the massacre, Kozakov was Dimitri's guest, and in order to feed the ataman's table they were slaughtering the Jews' cows and goats in Dimitri's yard. Tolia Shabolinski, the "sacrifice for the Jews,"[65] continued to grab the Jews' chickens, chopping off their heads and handing them to the Jewish women to cook lunch for the "guests," and at the same time she consoled them that the "guests" were going to leave soon.

The village was still in holiday spirits. The local bandits were still wearing their inside-out jackets with the backward-facing hats, and tied up their beards and forelocks so that they would not be recognized, and the Gentile girls, dressed up in their Sunday clothes with beads and ribbons, were dancing drunkenly in every yard, showing off the rings and bracelets on their hands. There in the Gentile streets the music did not stop playing, they were still getting drunk and gorging themselves at the set tables on all sorts of good things, singing and playing on their balalaikas and harmonicas, and the Gentiles' despicable laughter still echoed over the survivors in the shtetl.

Frequently local and out-of-town bandit youth came with questions to the Jewish women and children who were in Shabolinski's storehouse, "Who is your God? Lenin or Trotsky?" And one of them demanded that the little Jewish children kiss him and when they clung in fear to their mothers, he yelled out that he would throw them all alive into the lime pits. The women, with their frightened children around them, begged him and kissed his hands until he gave in, and then he left the shelter quietly. These human-beasts already had their fill of slaughters and murders. They were still dragging girls and women off to be raped. They tore off the dirty bonnets and kerchiefs from the dark and blonde heads of those who were made-up and disguised as old women, but they no longer took their souls. The local and out-of-town bandits were already tired of robbery and blood. By then Moyshe the wheelwright was certainly able to think of something to do.

The first thing he did was count his children. All six including Khananye were sitting in Shabolinski's shelter, huddling in a corner near their crying mother. She was missing the seventh child. It was in fact the small six-year-old boy who did not want to separate from his mother. By force she tore him from herself and sent him crying with her older girl to the cellar of Berislavsky the furrier, because she was afraid that there were too many children with her.

But she had protected her two birds well. Her husband's community earnings were enough for her to have Yossel the furrier take the children with him to his "secret" place, because it was secure. The entire summer he and two other

Jews, his relatives, dug underground in his cellar, and there they built a truly clever hiding place. It was a room with all the conveniences for people to live. Air to breathe and rays of light streamed through the invisible cracks punched through from above, and the entrance was so cleverly disguised that the owners themselves had to make markings for how to get inside.

This particular "secret" place was well known in Dubova, and many people wanted to safeguard themselves there when the evil moment of mortal danger came. So they reserved places in Berislavsky's cellar which, like tickets for a performance, would be announced at the right time. But not everybody was one of the lucky ones, because the dug-out cellar room was not excessively large. In addition, Yossel the furrier himself had a big family and he wanted all of his relatives to be near him.

Everyone conducted themselves this way everywhere. People used their last bit of strength in the cruel moments of mortal danger and fear of death, so that all their relatives could stay together, in order to be able to communicate their last wishes to each other. Whoever survived would know what to do with the remaining property, or take care of a widow with orphans, and if everybody were killed they would all be buried together in a Jewish cemetery.

This was also the ideal of the well-established and wealthy furrier Yoysef Berislavsky. That's why he and his relatives worked arduously the entire summer to dig underground. He wanted in life and death to protect himself, his household and his large family.

But during the great massacre in Dubova there was no hiding place. His concealed room under the walls of the cellar was discovered Thursday during the day, when a child there started to cry, and nobody knows how they killed nine families, because the only witnesses were the mute walls, soaked with blood and marrow of Jewish individuals. The fourteen-year-old daughter of Moyshe the wheelwright, who miraculously ran into the street, remembered nothing to tell. She immediately had a frightening nervous breakdown and somewhere stumbled into a yet-still-standing destroyed home with broken windows and doors. She lay there that night amidst ripped-up pillows and broken dishes, and in the morning a Gentile woman happened to hear her hysterical cries and brought the girl by the hand into Shabolinski's storehouse, but her little brother remained among the bones and skulls of the Berislavsky family whom the Gentiles later flung into the lime pits.

But the dead child did not evoke a single tear from Moyshe.

36

At this time Moyshe was fully occupied with those who were alive. He immediately sent messengers to the surrounding shtetls to get help for the Dubova widows and orphans. Two hired horsemen who rode out were from the few peasant families who during the massacre hid Jews in their homes. The peasant Senia Ringatsh was the hero of these two Dubova righteous and pious Gentiles. Both of them along with their wives pretended to be bandits, so they would not be suspected of being friendly to Jews, and that is how they saved many women and children.

On Friday night as Kozakov and his staff were heading out of town with singing and music, accompanied by the enthusiastic peasant youth through the Gentile streets, Dimitri Shabolinski saddled a horse to ride to Uman with a letter from Moyshe the wheelwright to the Uman rabbi for help on behalf of the hungry women and children of Dubova.

He, Dimitri the shoemaker, had traveled the world, was a sophisticated, citified man, and in the first days of the Revolution he was also a free thinker——he understood how to play both sides in the pitiless time of civil war. During the days and nights of the massacre, when the surrounding peasant population helped Kozakov's army slaughter the Jewish shtetl, Kozakov, along with his staff, was Dimitri's guest, and he fed him in his home with all sorts of good things that his "soldiers" brought from Jewish houses and stores.

Afterward when the Dubova community of Jews was already lying in the lime pits and the stone hearts of the Gentile mothers began to tremble for the Jewish infants, Dimitri proposed that they ring the church bells and request putting a stop to killing any more women and children, for whom he was providing his house as a safe haven. He immediately drew red crosses on his windows and doors, so it would signify for the local bandits that it was a neutral rescue station of the Red Cross. And if a strict unit of the Red punitive brigade dropped in on the shtetl, the Jewish widows and orphans would protect him like a savior angel who had saved their lives from murderous hands.

As such, Dimitri also went to the representatives of the Uman Jewish community with Moyshe the wheelwright's letter in his hand.

But the Uman Jews were then barely able to help the Dubova widows and orphans, because their heads were under the sword twenty-four hours a day. The city was besieged on all sides by hordes of bandits, and a few hundred Jewish youth, armed with raucous old Berdan rifles, were battling against them. These were the same Jewish youth who had earlier hid from mobilization into the Red Army, and after the "quiet" massacre in Uman they decided it was better to die as Bolsheviks in battle with the enemy than let themselves be slaughtered like sheep in their quiet attics.

But Shabolinski did not leave Uman empty-handed. He related to the Uman Jewish community leaders a small part of the Jewish chronicle of Dubova, and they began trembling. They tore away a bite of bread from their own widows and orphans, who themselves were wandering around fainting in the streets, and Dimitri brought 10,000 Kerensky rubles to Moyshe the wheelwright.

It was already Saturday morning. The twenty-six Jewish men who survived in the shtetl were still lying hidden in the attics, because once again at night there was an uproar. Petliura's Ataman Pavlov and his troops came into Dubova. They even emphatically ordered that the Jews not hide, and whoever dared to do such a thing would be harshly punished, as it would be an insult to the Ukrainian army if the peaceful inhabitants did not trust them. Nonetheless the Jews were afraid to show themselves in Dimitri's yard.

And Moyshe the wheelwright was wandering in the street, watching how the local Gentiles were still carrying the Jewish dead to the lime pits at the base of the mountain. Also on Saturday morning they dragged out of the water the drowned Etel Olshanitsky and Ayzik Tshernov, who ran from the murderers' hands into the river. Afterward in the street Etel's daughter was screaming and imploring that the Jews bury her mother—so that no dogs would drag her around. But nobody wanted to risk their lives to go to the cemetery. Even the Jewish smiths and their wives and children were afraid to show themselves outside their doors. They too were by then in Shabolinski's storehouse. On Friday night as it started to get dark, they had suddenly been seized by a fear of the lime pits, which were located below the fences of their yards, so they began to leave their very comfortable houses and ran with their wives and children to join the widows and orphans in the dark space on Dimitri's property.

It was cramped and hot in there. Many children were sick with dysentery, because for three days in a row they had been given dry wheat kernels peeled off the stalks to eat in the field. There was no way they could quiet the two orphan infants. One was Sarah Nimerovsky's tiny child, for whose sake the miracle occurred that they stopped killing women and children, and the other was the first-born of a murdered young couple. This child was also being carried alive to the lime pits and the curious Gentile women who were standing there had pity on it and carried it back into the shtetl. All the women rocked and caressed these two tiny children, but none of the nursing Jewish women had even a drop of milk to give them. They were all shrunken, and their milk had disappeared out of fear. The Gentile women then did a good deed for them. When night fell a few of the women of means from the Gentile streets brought to Dimitri's storehouse pieces of bread and pitchers of fresh milk for the children.

But Saturday morning they were all once again sitting in a faint, and Dimitri with his 10,000 rubles from Uman was truly like an angel from heaven.

On the same day, help from Torgovitsa and the nearby shtetl Pokotilov also came. Jews risked their lives and in great danger they brought two wagons of bread for the Dubova widows and orphans, and on Sunday Jews from Talne brought bread and a sack of millet with a little sugar. And in the sack of millet was hidden money, 2,000 rubles.

Also the Talne messengers told Moyshe the wheelwright that an additional ten householders from their shtetl would risk their lives to travel along the road where the bandits were ambushing Jews in wagons and on foot. Ten Talne Jews would come with shrouds and talleisim, at least enough for the rabbi and son and for the old people who were lying in the pits, and they would help take the dead from the lime pits and bring them to be buried in a Jewish cemetery.

Moyshe heard them out and immediately went to the new leader of the militia to inform him that in accordance with Jewish law those who were murdered had to be taken from the pits and brought to the cemetery to be buried.

But he got angry and answered him sharply, "Moshke, I don't advise you to take this on. Thank God that you yourself survived, and now watch yourself. The village will tear you to pieces. In such hot weather, do you want to bring on a plague? Is it revenge you want, Moshke? Watch yourself. They let you live …"

But Moyshe also answered him very seriously, "Me? Can such a small person take revenge for an entire city of murdered people? You mock me!"

At these words, the militia leader became softer. "So Moshke, people are sinful, God must forgive them. But nobody has anything against you."

Moyshe the wheelwright couldn't speak any further with him. He swallowed the tears that were stuck in his throat and went back to the Talne messengers with a clear answer, that the Dubova Jews couldn't be buried in a Jewish cemetery because the Gentiles were afraid of a plague. And, when the widows began to cry loudly, he added spontaneously that the lime pits were an abyss, in whose depths everything sank, and the corpses simply couldn't be taken out of there. At that moment a thought struck him, that everything was over. The Dubova Jewish community was already entirely erased from the earth, and he had to escape with his wife and children somewhere to seek out a new home.

And then he set about saving the twenty-three Torah scrolls that were still intact in the Dubova synagogues. There was not a single window remaining in the study house, and the small synagogue was standing with its broken doors wide open. Above in the women's section of the synagogue sixteen people were killed on the first night of the massacre, and the white walls were sprayed red, as if they were under a rain of blood. Moyshe and his son Khananye, with two other young men of the Talne messengers, tried not to step on the shreds of the ripped-up holy books and the rivulets of dried blood that looked like they were from slaughtered oxen. Also flecked with blood were the Torah scrolls with their mantles torn off and their silver pointers detached.

All twenty-three Torahs were packed in boxes and sent with the messengers to Talne, and the Talne Jews were afraid to take the silver Torah breastplate with them that they found under the bimah. So Moyshe wrapped it in a torn tallis and buried it in the synagogue yard until it could be dug up and brought to a holy place in a living Jewish community.

37

But for the Dubova Jews their cup of anguish was still not full. Before they could leave their dead shtetl, they still had a lot to go through.

Sunday, when the Talne Jews rode off with the Torah scrolls from the Dubova synagogues, the Jewish widows and orphans once more experienced the fear of death. Petliura's Ataman

Zeleny[66] came through with a few hundred horsemen and infantry dressed in baggy blue trousers with tasseled knitted belts with Ukrainian yellow and blue flags. Immediately the few men ran into the hiding places, and the women and children locked the doors of Shabolinski's storehouse and squeezed together in the darkness afraid to breathe. But the Ukrainian troops under Petliura's Ataman Zeleny, who in the Ivanki shtetl forced the Jews to eat the glass of their broken windows, were very magnanimous toward the Jewish population of Dubova. The destroyed shtetl, with its blood-stained walls and severed human limbs lying around in the streets was so gruesome that it made an impression on Ataman Zeleny's "soldiers."

They stopped near Shabolinski's house with the red crosses on the windows and doors and asked, "Why are they keeping the Jewish women and orphans locked in? One even gives air to breathe to cattle and wild beasts." So then Dimitri opened the storehouse and told the Jewish women and children that they had nothing to be afraid of: well-disciplined troops were coming, who everywhere established the unwavering authority of the people in the Ukrainian Republic. The ataman ordered the mothers and children to go out into the street to have a look at these true Ukrainian soldiers.

The boys started to run out first as if from a cage and after them the terror-stricken mothers. But the men were still afraid to show themselves, and so they spent the night in the attics because as they were leaving, the well-disciplined Ukrainian troops of Petliura's Ataman Zeleny covered the village streets with proclamations: "Beat up Jews and Save Ukraine!"

It was Sunday evening. On the next day, around noon, another wagon with bread came from Talne. The messenger brought a receipt from the Talne rabbi for the twenty-three Torah scrolls from Dubova. He also wrote that they should hire at his expense two wagons from the Gentiles and send fifty orphans to him in the shtetl. The Talne Jews would take it upon themselves to feed them, provide them with shoes and clothes, and give them an education as if they were their own children.

The orphans, mostly the young boys, were very happy about this journey. Moyshe the wheelwright hired two peasant wagons for 7,000 rubles of Ukrainian money, and whichever children were the most dexterous jumped aboard the wagons. Sitting one on top of the other, the noisy, happy Dubova orphans traveled to Talne.

But in the evening they all came back to the shtetl, frightened and crying. Driving through the village of Madanovsk, eight versts from Talne, a horseman came to them and told them that bandits had attacked Talne and were robbing and killing there. The children began to cry heavily and begged the wagoners to bring them back to Dubova. The Gentiles had pity on them and brought them back home, but they demanded of Moyshe the wheelwright their 7,000 rubles for travel money.

Moyshe was desperate. He showed them the note from the Talne rabbi that his community would pay for the wagons and begged them to wait until there was some news from there, but they threatened him with the local young bandits who would settle accounts with Moyshe for this. Moyshe realized that this was bad, so he turned to Brishko to calm down the two wagoners until he could pay them for the wagons.

And Markela was feeling so generous that he settled this matter in favor of Moyshe the wheelwright. He ordered the two peasants to wait until Moyshe had the community money to pay the debt.

In these days after the great massacre, Markela once again undertook his guardianship of the shtetl. The national committees of the Ukrainian partisans had already overthrown the Kyiv Directorate, and Brishko was appointed by them to fulfill his obligations as commander and to protect the peaceful population.[67] Also Feyge-Vitele had already become a skilled horse-rider, so he, Brishko, was able to devote time to keeping order in Dubova, and therefore he gave Moyshe the wheelwright and two other young Jews a few of his soldiers as assistants to help remove the human bones and skulls from the streets.

38

The energetic Jewish community councilman from Dubova's narrow streets had nothing else to do than devote himself to burials. For entire days Moyshe wandered around the shtetl with his assistants, collecting into sacks severed hands and feet, ears, noses, and heads with hats, braids, and combs from the rubbish and dust in the streets. And inside the houses Moyshe found body parts and individual limbs of people right out in the open on chairs and tables, in beds among feathers and torn rags, and in vessels for cooking and washing.

Also Moyshe had a task to fill in the collapsed cellar in the middle of the market into which they had thrown eight people along with the Koretskys. Once a ray of sun stole through the wreckage in the cellar and they saw an arm dressed in one of Gishe Koretsky's jackets. Moyshe then called together a minyan and they filled in the cellar. With a minyan they also buried in the cemetery the sacks of heads and bones collected from the streets, and the minyan also had to go to the lime pits every day. They would regularly find there, among the carcasses of horses and cattle thrown there by the Dubova peasants, murder victims with obvious traces of people they knew.

For entire days Moyshe the wheelwright was engaged in this way with communal work relating to the dead Jewish congregation. But as soon as night fell he went to hide in a corner of Shabolinski's storehouse near his sleeping children and listened to the women's stories and miracles about how each one of them was saved from death. His wife was still crying over her small child who didn't want to separate from her, who she herself had forced away out of fear that she had too many children with her. But as soon as it got dark she, just like the rest of the women, was afraid to take a step out the door. Fear also gripped the children. They used to scare each other with the lime pits and with the empty synagogues where the corpses prayed at night, and therefore they, the orphans, were afraid to go there in the morning to say Kaddish[68] for their murdered fathers and mothers.

Also the crazy Mindl Posternak sang out from the smashed-up small synagogue. During the great massacre she even danced in the middle of the marketplace, and the Gentile market-goers were amused by her dancing, accompanying her on harmonicas. She would even be seen dancing near the lime pits. An out-of-town crazy woman with a child at her side who had escaped from somewhere and wandered into Dubova was clapping along with her. They said the child was not hers. After they had killed her children, she stole the child from an orphanage in Uman. During the day both crazy women along with the child would roam around the Gentile streets. They would nourish themselves with the pieces of bread that the Gentile women parceled out to them out of pity, and at night they would sit somewhere in a destroyed Jewish house and with their Yiddish and Ukrainian songs would cheer up the surrounding Gentile neighbors.

On the quiet summer evenings even the fortunate Dubova Jewish smiths who used to be afraid to sleep in their undamaged homes were singing. In the village they used to get drunk along with the Gentiles in the Gentile taverns, singing Gentile songs.

Also singing during the enchanted moonlit Ukrainian nights with their fragrant breath of ripe orchards and gardens was Shkodnik's granddaughter, the gentle and exquisitely beautiful Etele. In the days of the massacre the bandits dragged her father and mother and their younger children from their hiding place in the yard of Brishko's parents. In the moment of danger, he, Berl the cantor, with his wife and children, ran to his Gentile in-laws. And they, the in-laws, along with their surrounding neighbors, pleaded with Ataman Kozakov himself for Berl the cantor and his family, invoking Feyge-Vitele's importance and Kozakov spared the lives of Brishko's in-laws, despite the fact that on the battlefield Kozakov was Brishko's enemy.

Etele was hidden by her good Christian friends, the former police superintendent Yanovich and his wife. After the massacre she never returned to her grandfather's beautiful empty house.

As she herself was so unhappy, she was estranged from her selfish and happily in-love sister. Etele was still in love with the quiet, dreamy Andriusha, who in the days of the great massacre was sitting with a book in his hand on his father's porch under the old fragrant linden trees, and he was listening to the lamenting screams and the anguished death throes of those being tortured to death. He finally listened to his father and stopped meeting with her, so Etele remained at the Yanoviches. There she used to get drunk and sing through the night along with the priest's sons, the robber-students, and the feldsher Deviatkin, who would cleverly imitate how the wounded Jewish women cried in the hospital when he consoled them that they would soon die.

39

And Moyshe the wheelwright was still thinking about how to escape from the dead shtetl. The few remaining householders, widows, and orphans did not let Moyshe out of their sight. They all started selling their houses, but the Gentiles did not want to buy every house. Many Jewish buildings were already destroyed. They were not at all eager to buy any old and small homes. They only bought the new and intact buildings, and for absolutely next to nothing, because they had no need for them. Besides, they realized that everything was about to be in their possession anyway. And if they did pay money for the Jewish houses, requiring official contracts with signatures from the Jewish community council on behalf of the underage orphans, it was only out of fear that at another time the bandits would turn their jackets inside-out and the Reds would storm in once again with their punitive brigade.

But leaving the shtetl was still not an option. All the roads that led to the larger Jewish cities were being watched by bandits. A few times the Dubova women and children tried to travel on the busy Uman highway towards the city where the Dubova heder boys used to run on foot long ago. But each time they had to turn back, because everywhere they came upon Jewish corpses hanging from the trees on both sides of the road or sprawled in the fields, blackened by the sun and gnawed at by dogs.

They still had to wait a long time for the right moment when they could run away from the ruins and the graves. But suddenly there happened to be a lucky opportunity, and a few people at least were able to leave the shtetl.

It was one day at dawn.

On the sixth day after the great massacre a short sailor came to Dubova and began asking about a Jewish girl named Sosye. This was the well-known beautiful step-daughter of old Getsl Portigul, whom they killed because of her in the cellar of the zemstvo post office during the "small" massacre. This particular sailor then stole her from his friends, the bandits, and brought her to the village to a Gentile's house, asking them to guard the Jewish girl because she was his fiancée. He said he would come for her in a few days. But he came two months later, because he hid out in the villages so that he would not be seen by Kozakov's "soldiers" from under whose noses he took away the beautiful Jewish woman.

Tolia Shabolinski brought this particular person into the storehouse to the Jewish women and children, saying lightheartedly, "This man is looking for the girl Sosye, tell him where she lives."

The women exchanged glances with one another, and everyone remained silent. But Tolka, "the sacrifice for the Jews," immediately admonished them all. "Foolish women, why are you silent? He says that if you do not give him Sosye he will call his boys over ... Do you need all this now?"

Hearing such clear words, the women became talkative. They started asking among themselves where Sosye was, and a little girl called out that she knew where Sosye was. She was living with her mother far away in the village in a small Gentile house among the gardens. She could point out where it was.

A few agile women grabbed their crying children by the hand and ran off with the girl, looking for the hiding place of

Basye Portigul and her daughter. Meanwhile they asked Tolka to give food and vodka to the sailor and to keep him at home until they came back.

The misfortune befell Basye so unexpectedly.

After the "small" massacre of the 20th of Sivan, Basye and her girl left the ground floor of the zemstvo post office with its corpse cellar where they kept finding people's bones, and the two of them settled among the peasant gardens in a tiny house on land rented to them out of pity by a kind Gentile. For the entire summer Basye guarded Sosye with her life. She applied all kinds of salves to her wounded and bruised body, and bathed her in tubs of grasses and herbs that the neighborhood Gentile women gave her as a remedy. And God helped her: Sosye became healthy and beautiful once again. Both of them worked on the kind Gentile's land in his distant orchards. And this was how the mother hid the young woman during the days of the great massacre, so that not a single impure glance from any bandit youth would fall on her.

But one morning a group of women called her out to tell her a terrible secret.

Basye wrung her hands and asked in anguish and tears, "Why specifically my sacrifice? I have already paid my dues ..."

"He only wants Sosye ..."

"Specifically Sosye? Specifically my sacrifice? ...," she stammered like someone who was doomed.

But the group of women beleaguered her from all sides with words from their pearly lips from the *Tsene-rene*[69] and tkhine: "And Esther the Queen, what did she do? She was so beautiful and proper like your Sosye. Saving so many people from death, is this a small thing? By her virtue the memory of Dubova will live on. The orphans will grow up and for generations they will tell about this, her name will be written in the holy books, like the name of Queen Esther ... bestow on your child this virtue ..."

"But my sacrifice, but my sacrifice!" she continued to plead desperately, and with these words she threw herself at the door of her small home. Her tearful voice trembled in a stern call to her daughter.

Sosye remained standing at the doorstep, a frightened girl, because of the group of women that were whispering in secret with her mother.

"Dear daughter," Basye cried out once again devastated, "A bandit came and wants to take you from me, if not, he is going to kill all of the widows and orphans. My child, what do you have to say about this?"

"Is he dressed like a sailor?" the girl asked quietly.

"Like a sailor! Like a sailor!" the women entered the house in amazement, because she admitted recognizing him.

"A short man with thick lips?"

"Yes—yes!" They became even happier.

"So, it is him!" Sosye nodded her head and she told the truth, how during the "small" massacre the bandits fought over her. They wanted to shoot her, and he saved her from death, but she had to promise that she would convert and marry him.

Hearing these last words, Basye burst into tears, lamenting as if from a tkhine her living sacrifice.

But the happy women were no longer listening to her. They immediately ran to Shabolinski to get the sailor.

A few days later the short Moldovan with the sailor hat was united with Sosye in the Gentile house, and her mother Basye Portigul was also there with them. Sosye would walk in the street with him, and she introduced him to the Jewish girls and women that they ran into. In addition she told everyone that her groom was a respectable man. He had his own house and a grocery store in Tiraspol. He also had an elderly mother and a very nice sister there. He was forced to go off with Kozakov's bandits, but now he had stolen away and escaped from them.

Sosye also went along with her groom to the priest for him to convert her. Along with them were also a few Gentile neighbor women, and the telephone operator Yelena Vasiliyevna, who considered the sailor as a protégé because of his connection with her dear friend, Ataman Kozakov.

But the priest did not want to convert her for the same reason he did not convert Feyge-Vitele. It was truly a dangerous action after the entire shtetl full of Jews was massacred. The Red "demon" could come and with the blink of an eye could immediately ask the Orthodox priest why he was converting Jewish girls and marrying them to bandits.

And the priest did not let himself be convinced by anybody. Even the requests of Yelena Vasiliyevna did not help.

Then the sailor decided to take his bride home.

There in Tiraspol he had a mother and a sister, and they would organize everything in the Pokrov church, where the priest was a local man. Afterward they would remain there to live. Sosye also agreed to this, but at the same time she wanted to safeguard her mother. They had decided to take the elderly woman along and, on the way, leave her with her married daughter in the shtetl of Torgovitsa.

Basye herself liked the plan. First of all, she would be spared the pleasure of seeing how the Dubova Gentile girls and women would adorn Sosye with beads and ribbons and lead her with the icon into the church. Also the hope still blossomed in her that there in Torgovitsa she would be able to save the girl from his murderous hands. On the other side of the river was the famous Novoarkhangelsk district with its respectable Russian bastards who stuck up for the Jews. They had pelted Kozakov with bombs. They went around the shtetls looking for bandits, taking revenge for Jewish blood, so wouldn't they be able to defeat this insignificant little sailor?

As soon as she arrived at her daughter's she would enlist two or three respectable householders from Torgovitsa and would go with them across the river into this district. There in the market she was going to call together all of the important Russian bastard merchants with their sons, the Bolsheviks, who stood up for the Jews, and she would ask them to save her daughter. She would say that their faith didn't concern her, God was one for all of us, but why did her righteous beautiful child deserve to fall into the hands of a bandit? They, the decent Gentiles, would certainly have pity on her and would tear the little bandit to shreds like a herring.

This is what Basye came up with and in great secrecy told only the rebbetzin, who was lying in the hospital with a sewn-up, bandaged head.

Meanwhile in the shtetl there was a commotion regarding the secured wagon that would travel to Torgovitsa under the protection of Sosye's own bandit. He was a familiar man by then, and he would politely greet all the women to whom his Jewish bride had introduced him. So a group of women once more flung themselves at Basye with pleas to take them along, just like a few days earlier when they convinced her that her Sosye was as important a personality as Queen Esther.

But Basye had one contention, "We can't take everybody, so first let's ask the Gentile how many people he can take."

So they ran to the peasant from whom they rented the wagon. God performed a miracle and he agreed to travel with both of his wagons along with his son, and aside from the bride and groom and the old woman he could take six more people. But then there was again a turmoil, everybody wanting to be one of the six lucky passengers.

In the end they cast lots, and the six people were the wife of Zalmen the glazier with three small children and another Jewish woman with her only son, a thirteen-year-old. Neither of them needed to go to Torgovitsa, but the Jewish woman with the young son had to go to Kyiv to get help writing a letter, because her husband and a few children were already in America and it was said that in Kyiv there were American committees that sent letters over to America, and Zalmen the glazier still had to remain in Dubova in order to collect the money that was owed to him by the Gentiles. She, Zalmen's wife, along with her children availed themselves of the secure ride to escape from the bandits' nest. There was an open road from Torgovitsa to Yelisavetgrad, and from there one could make one's way to Odesa.

So on a beautiful morning in Elul[70] the two wagons left Dubova under the envious eyes of the remaining women and children. As they traveled through the oak woods near the village of Oksanyna, eight versts from the shtetl, both wagons were attacked by a group of young bandits with shooting from all sides. Once again there was fighting over Sosye. They were the "soldiers" of Kozakov, who were in Dubova during the "small" massacre when the short sailor took the beautiful Jewish girl right out of their hands. They had been searching for him in the surrounding villages for the entire summer, and they tracked him down when he came into the shtetl for her. Afterward they were waiting on the road to catch him and her together.

But the short Moldovan heroically stood up against them. Also helping him were the wagoner and a few other village youths that came running from Oksanyna, and Sosye remained his. He and she jumped onto the first wagon, and the wagoner cracked a whip at the horses, tearing up the earth beneath it.

They killed only five "lucky" people who wanted to flee from Dubova in time, and Sosye's mother Basye Portigul was the sixth. The only survivor was the wife of Zalmen the glazier. When night fell she snuck out from under the corpses, where she was lying wounded. Without a tear she kissed her three dead little children all over, and in the darkness of night she went through the harvested fields back to Dubova.

The next day an old Jewish woman from the village of Oksanyna risked her life. She dressed herself like a Gentile woman and went on foot to the shtetl of Pokotilov to tell them about the misfortune that happened on the road with the women and children of Dubova. The Pokotilov Jews sent a Gentile with a wagon, and they brought the six corpses into the shtetl, and on the following day they buried them in the Pokotilov Jewish cemetery.

40

After the incident with Sosye's steadfast bandit, the women from Dubova became a bit more patient about leaving the shtetl. The kind Dimitri Shabolinski moved them, the Jewish widows, into the three best Jewish houses because it was too crowded in his storehouse. He also couldn't stand the noise. Nonetheless he allowed around thirty Jewish souls to stay with him, because he really did not feel like parting with the red crosses on his windows and doors.

Moyshe the wheelwright and his family were also together with the widows and the orphans in those houses of the Jewish community. His home was still standing, but the insides were destroyed. The ripped-up bedding and broken dishes created an atmosphere of terror. So Khananye boarded up the windows and hung a lock on the door. He gathered together the bit of wood that remained near the workshop and handed it over to Dimitri to keep in his yard for a while. Moyshe was absolutely ready to leave, and, while observing him, the remaining community once again was feverish to flee from the ruins and graves as fast as possible.

Meanwhile the Dubova householder, Avrom-Moyshe Zaytshik, who even before the "small" massacre had fled to Uman, made his way back to the shtetl from there. While in Uman, upon hearing that the Dubova widows were selling their houses and that everybody wanted to leave town, he risked his life to travel the Uman highway to come persuade them not to sell their own spots. They should stay in place. Everybody should settle onto one street for the time being, and it should remain a Jewish community. Later, when there was once again a free bright world for everybody, those who had run away would return home, as it was not good at all to be homeless and wandering abroad.

There were people who agreed with him. The idea of allowing oneself to go on the road, stark naked, with the few numbered groschen from their sold homes, truly inspired fear in them. But Moyshe the wheelwright did not let them change his mind. He could not stay in Dubova and live once again as neighbors of the "decent" Gentiles who had helped the out-of-town bandits slaughter the entire shtetl of Jews with all types of humiliating deaths, and the majority of those who survived the great massacre were with him.

Meanwhile in the village they heard that Moyshe the wheelwright was seriously about to leave, and if anyone needed to fix an axle or mount a pair of wheels, he would have to drive a wagon into the city. So coming out of church on Sunday the oldest and finest householders from the Gentile streets convened a meeting and they called Moyshe to discuss a very important issue with him. And when he came, all of the Dubova peasants unanimously asked him to remain living there and the rest of the people could also remain in their places. They were guaranteeing that what had happened before would never happen again.

But Moyshe the wheelwright answered them very seriously that he could not trust their words, because their power as the peasant authority was not solid and before their very eyes they allowed the extermination of all the Jewish men, women, and children, and therefore he could not remain living there.

This particular peasant gathering took place under the open sky near the cooperative. Moyshe said his piece and was ready to walk away. But at that instant more people arrived from the village streets, and among them was the peasant Kedimon, who during the time of the ataman was a militiaman in Dubova, and afterward, when the Bolsheviks arrested him as a counter-revolutionary, the Jews pleaded on his behalf and with their signatures freed him. In that moment he came with his resolute idea, and he told off the group in clear words, "Why do you have to beg him to stay? Don't you know what they are doing to Jews in other places? They are slaughtering them until the last one, and we will also do this."

In a dead silence these words were heard by the entire peasant gathering. But the stiff broken voice of the Jewish worker Moyshe the wheelwright was the only one to speak up: "You will not kill off all the Jews. For this reason, God has scattered us throughout the world for us to live forever. If we are all slaughtered in Ukraine, we will survive in America, in Germany, in Poland, in other countries, but you should know that there will be no good end for you either. There will come those who will kill you off too. The blood of our small children will answer you back."

The surrounding group stood there quietly and pensively bowed their heads. Even the ataman's former militiaman was silent, and without saying a word they all dispersed and went home to their little white houses planted with greenery on the blossoming Gentile streets. The few Jews there were still fuming. In that minute Moyshe the wheelwright was accosted with harsh complaints from all three Jewish community houses about why he answered back to the Gentiles so vehemently, but he answered them firmly too, "Whoever wants to remain living in Dubova should seek another community councilman."

41

On Sunday during the day Moyshe the wheelwright was discussing things with the Dubova peasants, and in the evening, reliable information came into the shtetl, that Kozakov was once again near Dubova. Kozakov had stopped in the nearby village of Babanka, and nobody knew where he would go after that. Brishko and Feyge-Vitele, who were comfortably living in Shkodnik's opulent home, immediately ran away from the shtetl along with his soldiers, taking with him the duties of the Kyiv Directorate along with Feyge-Vitele's bicycle and her sleek saddled riding horses.

Meanwhile the local bandits let Kozakov and his "general staff" know that the Dubova Jewish widows had sold their houses and they now had a lot of Nikolai money, and so he immediately came with a few hundred armed horsemen once again to loot out the ruins of the Jewish shtetl. It only lasted one hour in broad daylight, as the local peasants were returning calmly from the field bringing their ripened grain into their barns. The local peasants did not get involved this time, and in that one bright sunny hour in the middle of the day Kozakov and his bandits killed eight people, raped many women and little girls, and took the money from the widows that they had received for their houses.

The nostalgic Dubova resident Avrom-Moyshe Zaytshik, who at the risk of life and limb had come running from Uman to dissuade them from disturbing the Jewish community of Dubova, was also killed in this latest slaughter. Also this time Moyshe the wheelwright paid with the best and most precious of what he had. They even killed his darling, his comfort and his hope, his sensitive Khananye.

During the entire summer of the Jewish massacres in Dubova Khananye was always within Moyshe's sight. Throughout all the misfortunes the mother and small children would lock themselves into their house and he, the sixteen-year-old Khananye, was always standing near his father, who would be running around looking for sympathizers among the militia and Gentile committee men to help him come to an agreement with the ataman.

This time, when the bandits were invading the Jewish houses, Moyshe stood in front of the door of the Jewish community home where he was hiding with his wife and children. In his arms he was holding his little boy, and Khananye was inside next to his mother. Upon seeing through the open door the wild riders roiling through the town, he started to run outside to his father, but his mother blocked the way with her hand. In that instant the bandits attacked the home with the girls and women. It became a frightening pandemonium. The cries of those being raped shook the walls, and in that particular storm Moyshe lost sight of his Khananye.

He had run out into the street and near the cooperative he mixed in among the peasants who out of curiosity were standing there. But at that minute near Shabolinski's garden someone killed Shapiro the cantor and his wife, who had run to hide in Dimitri's yard. Khananye got scared and ran out into the field. He encountered a bandit horseman with his gun held high, but the bandit rode past him. Next to the road there were Dubova peasant children standing in the reaped fields grazing the sheep. The horseman turned to them and asked where the Jews were hiding.

"That one is a Jew," the children pointed at Khananye.

The boy became courageous and stood there. This raised a doubt in the bandit youth. Moreover, Khananye was wearing his cap with the symbolic crest of the Gymnasium and his clean chintz overshirt that his mother had just pressed and dressed him in that morning.

"No, he doesn't look like a Jew," the bandit said perplexedly, "So, say the prayer."

Khananye recited word for word the Christian morning prayer, "Our Father," which he had heard plenty of times from his peasant neighbors' children.

"Cross yourself," the other one ordered again.

And Khananye crossed himself perfectly.

The peasant children burst out laughing and all began yelling in one voice that he was a Jewish boy whose name was Khananye .... His father was named Moshke and he made wheels.

The horseman fired, and then rode off on the road to the bridge.

The bullet hit Khananye in his head and he immediately fell dead. The children ran right into the shtetl to tell this to his father ....

When the bandits left, Moyshe the wheelwright hired two peasant wagons to bring the seven corpses to the cemetery. All of them were men. The eighth, Khaye-Feyge the cantor's wife was still lying in the hospital fatally wounded, and in the morning, because there were no more Jews left, he and Dimitri hired three Gentiles to dig graves. The few that were still remaining were hiding in the Jewish community houses, dazed and devastated from fear and despair.

Aside from the Gentile gravediggers, at the burial there were also Shabolinski and the disconcerted and implacable Zekharye Kozodoy who also trailed after Moyshe. Zekharye was still dreaming about revenge for his two small children whom the local inside-out jackets had killed on the night of Pesach Sheni in Dovid the butcher's house.

Moyshe buried his Khananye by himself. He did not let his mother near him. In her corner of the Jewish community apartment, women were trying to revive her with drops. And Moyshe kissed Khananye all over his longish shot-through head with the half-open child-like eyes, and he tenderly laid him in his grave. Alone he filled the grave with dirt, said Kaddish and recited the "El Maleh Rachamim"[71] prayer.

And after the burial Moyshe placed seven sticks with carved names of the murder victims at the heads of all seven graves. He did the same thing on the third day, when he and Dimitri buried Khaye-Feyge the cantor's wife, who died of her wounds in the zemstvo hospital in immense pain.

42

On the fourth day after his son's burial, Moyshe the wheelwright and his wife and five children drove off from Dubova on a Gentile-driven wagon. He made for Holovanivsk, the shtetl of his birth, where all summer the young Jews had fought the bandits. With him he had a few saved groschen and something he was holding in trust for the community. Before he left, he dug up the silver Torah breastplate that he had buried in the synagogue yard wrapped in a tallis on the day that the Talne messengers took the Torah scrolls from the Dubova synagogues, and God showed him mercy. The Gentile wagoner brought him, his wife, and children to his old childhood home, and he gave the Torah breastplate to that shtetl's synagogue.

And that was how the destroyed shtetl was left with no one in charge of the Jewish community.

After Moyshe the wheelwright abandoned Dubova, the Jewish widows and orphans were entirely under the protection of Dimitri Shabolinski. Not for nothing was Shabolinski called "the zhid father" in the Gentile streets. During the last massacre, the Jewish women were robbed of the last bit of earnings they had received for selling their houses. They were living hungry, barefoot, devastated in the community apartments, and it was still dangerous to travel from the shtetl. So he, the good Gentile, cared for them. He would travel to Uman, to Talne, to Pokotilov, and each time he brought them a bit of food from those Jewish communities, who themselves were already ruined from robberies and killings.

He was a bit of a messenger from God, a father for the Jewish widows and orphans. He was then already standing guard to keep their bit of property intact. The money from the rest of the sold houses had already been handed over to Dimitri, and they also brought to his house what was left in the Jewish stores and their few valuable household objects that had still remained somewhere in a corner away from the robbers' hands. They had turned everything over to his custody in his honest Gentile domain until the danger on the roads was over and they were able to take it out of the shtetl.

Also remaining with Dimitri were the possessions of the cantor Shapiro. His wife Khaye-Feyge was herself a great woman of valor, and in Dubova she had a beautiful shop selling porcelain dishes. All these years she was good friends with Tolka, "the sacrifice for the Jews," and she also safeguarded her possessions with her. Already from the first massacre onward the clever and energetic cantor's wife kept all of her few possessions at the Shabolinskis'. Piece by piece she carried the merchandise from her store and whatever was valuable from her home over to Dimitri's storeroom. She put the money and the silverware and jewelry directly into Dimitri's hands. She absolutely could not part with her earrings, because she had worn them since she got married and was very attached to them.

After the great massacre Khaye-Feyge noticed that something was not quite in order with her possessions that were secured with Tolia and Dimitri, because during the second night of the massacre, while running from the rabbi's attic to hide at Shabolinski's house, his sixteen-year-old daughter urged

Khaye-Feyge to give her the earrings that she was wearing, otherwise she would not let her into the house. Naturally Khaye-Feyge the "Cossack"[72] did not give the earrings to the Gentile girl, so Tolia became very angry with the cantor's wife. And after the last massacre when Khaye-Feyge was lying in the zemstvo hospital, a wreck on her deathbed, Tolia was once again interested in Khaye-Feyge's earrings: Tolia asked the rabbi's daughter-in-law to ask Khaye-Feyge, while she was still in her right mind, where she had hidden them, and the daughter-in-law retorted, "Why do you want to know?" and the clever Tolia answered, "After all, we have to wrap her in shrouds and bury her, so from where else are we supposed to get the funds for this?"

But the enlightened Gentile shoemaker Dimitri Shabolinski did one good deed for the cantor of the Dubova synagogue. After Dimitri had received the cantor's entire wealth to guard, he did not allow them to kill him in his yard. He told the bandit to take him someplace else, and the bandit obliged.

Also during the last massacre Dimitri was protecting under the red crosses on his windows and doors the thirty Jewish widows and orphans that he was keeping in his storehouse shelter.

This was how Dimitri stood guard over the Jewish women and children, until the last minute when they departed the shtetl.

Around the middle of Elul, when in Uman the Ukrainians with inside-out jackets had calmed down a bit under the influence of the Kyiv Directorate, which was already dying in the poisoned atmosphere of the incoming black Tatar Denikin's regime, the "zhid father of Dubova" hired a few peasant wagons and sent the Jewish widows along with the orphans to Uman. They took with them to the city the old rebbetzin with the bandaged axed head wearing her blood-stained kerchief over it and also took with them the two crazy women with the child who used to sing and dance at the lime pits to the sounds of the harmonicas of the Dubova peasant youth. The next day Dimitri Shabolinski himself came and he brought the money from the last sold houses to the Dubova women and orphans. He brought every bit of it, to the last groschen. He even did the wounded rebbetzin a favor and took into his attic the rabbi's books from the broken shelves that were strewn around in his ravaged and blood-spattered study.

43

The women and children left Dubova a few days before Rosh Hashanah,[73] and during the Jewish holidays, the Dubova peasants tore down all the Jewish houses, cleared out the area, and plowed it to make fields and gardens. They also destroyed the Jewish cemetery: they burnt the tombstones, plowed the land and sowed it with winter wheat. They also burnt the Torah arks, benches, and tables from the two synagogues that were still standing with their shattered windows and broken doors.

And all of this was witnessed by the three Jewish smiths' families, who alone remained in Dubova in order to serve the contented Gentile streets with their smith work. But two families of the fortunate Dubova smiths could not bear it. Just before Sukkoth,[74] they abandoned their firmly established properties that had had their fill of abundance and earnings, and they fled to Uman to become homeless wanderers. Only one smith remained, Moyshe Rabinovitsh and his wife, and this man got drunk with the Gentiles in the Gentile taverns for a long time, until he, over a glass of vodka, sold the ruins of the study house for 2,500 rubles, and this money remained in the tavern. And the other Dubova synagogue was sold to the Gentiles by the Dubova horse-dealer Yitskhok Kortshun for 11,000 rubles. It happened on a Thursday on market day when he came to Dubova to buy horses, and he had a drink of vodka with his former Gentile neighbors. He also took the money for himself.

The Dubova exiles in Uman were fiercely enraged by this particular desecration of the Holy Name, so they called these two little local "lepers"[75] to the Uman rabbi for a religious ruling. But it was already the sad winter days when the Denikin soldiers were rampaging in Uman. Exactly at this moment they arrested the rabbi. New bands of vultures were moving into this unlucky city, and that it is how it remained.

During these mournful days of winter in the year 1919, when the powerless Denikin regime was amusing itself with its black drunken massacre dances in the Jewish cities and shtetls, Moyshe the wheelwright came from Holovanivsk to Dubova to sell his home and to take from Shabolinski the small amount of wood he had left with him.

In the shtetl there were a police superintendent and an out-of-town village policeman. The militia remained the same, and Brishko was living as a civilian in Dubova in Shkodnik's house that Feyge-Vitele alone inherited from her Jewish grandfather and grandmother. After the great massacre, her Jewish father and mother with their younger children ran to Holovanivsk, and her sister, the gentle and wonderfully beautiful Etele, out of the pain of Andriusha rejecting her, went off to Uman and there she became a military lady among the drunken nationalist officers of General Denikin. She would drink with them in the restaurants, and she rode around town with them in Russian national troikas, drowning out the mutely frightened Jewish streets with her wanton ringing laughter.

Dimitri Shabolinski was not doing bad either. He opened a store with the Jewish merchandise that the Dubova Jewish widows gave him to hide, and he was no longer a proletarian at his shoemaker's workbench. He used to answer the Jewish women that everything they had left with him was stolen. He gave Moyshe the wheelwright the same answer when he came to him for his bit of wood.

Moyshe's house was also destroyed. The furniture had been removed, the windows and the doors were broken. They even dug up the cellar. Only the bare beaten-up walls remained.

The two synagogues also looked wretched. He was barely able to recognize that the plowed and sowed field, where he not long ago buried Khananye with his bare hands, putting a stick with his carved-out name near his head, was once the Dubova Jewish cemetery.

Feeling depressed and devastated, he was in a hurry to leave behind the ruins of the former Jewish shtetl that same day. But suddenly they reminded him that he was once a Jewish community councilman there. While he was walking in the street, he was grabbed by the two Gentiles whom after the great massacre he had hired with two wagons to send the Dubova orphans to Talne, and who in the middle of the route had to turn around with the children because bandits had attacked Talne. So they asked him for the 7,000 rubles which he had then agreed upon. They threatened him with lynching if he did not pay them the money on the spot.

Moyshe was desperate. With great difficulty he convinced them to go with him to the volost for the village leader to hear out their grievances, and that he would abide by whatever he might say. But the village leader gave him a challenging task. He ordered him to travel with the Gentiles to Talne and ask the Talne Jews for the money, because they had signed a note that they would pay, and the two peasants forced him to travel with them to Talne.

But it was only there that he made it through this great anxiety. The Talne Jews did not deny the note, but as of then they had lived through so many killings and robberies that they could not pay the 7,000 rubles on the spot. But there was a Jew there who loaned the community the money, and the two Dubova peasants freed the arrested Moyshe the wheelwright whom they were threatening with a death sentence.

Moyshe never returned to Dubova again.

In Holovanivsk it was still destined for him to survive the Denikin massacre, and he couldn't bear the Jewish fear for one's life anymore. As soon as the Bolsheviks took back Ukraine, he and his six exhausted souls went to the happily Jewish Odesa that did not have experience with any Jewish sorrow or rage, because the city lay before an open sea with its windows and doors wide open to the cultural lands of Europe and America. There the Ukrainian and Russian nationalist patriots were ashamed to organize such days and nights of slaughter of Jews as they had done in the interior of the country.

It was already the summer of the year 1920.

44

At that time the Bolsheviks shot Markela Brishko. When he was under arrest in Uman, Feyge-Vitele went out among the Dubova homeless to get signatures on his behalf, that he, Markela, was a decent person, but the Dubova Jews did not want to give her any signatures. This time, when the shtetl and cemetery were already overgrown with blooming fields and gardens and they had also planted potatoes where the synagogues had stood—this time they could afford the luxury of not protecting any bandits with Jewish signatures.

Feyge-Vitele was therefore very angry at the Dubova Jews. But afterward she calmed herself down. After her husband's death she traveled back to Korzhova and became a Ukrainian language teacher at the local elementary school, and once again on market day in Dubova she would come dressed up in beads and ribbons, just like the Ukrainian peasant daughters. Before long Feyge-Vitele was even consoled in her lonely widowhood. Another pogrom-intellectual consoled her. He was the former Polish steward of the Korzhova upper-class estates, who was Brishko's capable collaborator in organizing the first Jewish massacre in Dubova, who fell in love with Markela's widow and married her.

Her joy was seen by the Dubova homeless, who also used to trudge every Thursday to Dubova to the market in order to earn a pittance for their expenses. Meanwhile they always had work in the lime pits, going with a minyan to cover up with earth the Jewish bones that had been exposed where the Gentiles used to get lime for coating their houses. But the Dubova Jews at the market were already accustomed to this. All of them were depressed, homeless, ragged, and hungry, and often they were envious of the dead.

Zekharye Kozodoy was still seeking to take revenge for the death of his two small children. Insulted and implacable, he was seeking a fair trial from the Soviet authority. He also pulled in for this particular undertaking two homeless youngsters from Dubova who during the great massacre lost their fathers and mothers along with brothers and sisters. And these particular plaintiffs cast a fear onto the Dubova Gentile streets. From the entire surrounding peasant community with its big villages and hamlets who were all participants in the robbery and murder of the Jewish population, Zekharye handed over to the Uman Cheka[76] a total of eight young bandits whom he blamed for the death of his small children. But they all were terrified. They all felt that their hands were soaked in the innocent Jewish blood of old people and infants that they slaughtered at their mother's breasts.

And therefore the large and rich peasant community of Dubova became afraid of the homeless wandering Jew Zekharye Kozodoy.

45

And Moyshe the wheelwright also remained unchanged. Upon coming to Odesa his weakness for community work was again awakened. He attempted to organize the thirty-two homeless families from Dubova that also ran away from the Ukrainian cities and shtetls into the blessed Jewish city near the open sea with its windows and doors opened towards the cultured lands of Europe and America.

Moyshe wanted to organize a kind of Dubova colony in Odesa, as a remembrance of their old home. To this end, he got in touch with the elders of the Shalashna synagogue[77] for them to give him money for expenses to bring the Dubova Torah scrolls from Talne and to organize within the Shalashna synagogue a Dubova minyan with their own shochet and a prayer leader who had fled here from Dubova.

But the plan never came about because the wealthy Shalashna synagogue, after the blaze caused by the fireball that had hit it in Elul 5679[78] when the Denikin army came into

Odesa, was itself homeless and greatly impoverished by the Soviet regime.

This remained merely a nice dream for the elderly Dubova kosher slaughterer, who was stuck, hungry, in an attic room along with his nine hungry children, and the tenth, their nervous frightened mother. Thirty-two families from the old home supported him, even though they were also hungry and were themselves stuck in dark cellars and in attic rooms just like he was.

Moyshe the wheelwright also lived in the darkness of a cellar, with his small workshop for lathing woodwork in the grey light of the window near the ground. His six weary and frightened souls couldn't stand the bright sunshine of the Odesa streets. So when they would come out of the darkness to the bright outdoors, the sun would drive them crazy. Everyone was nourished with pale tea and overbaked bran bread, and the blood of these seven people became as pale as water. Afterward their anemia reached the point where the smaller children were constantly sleeping. When their mother woke them up to put a piece of bread in their mouth to eat with a little bit of warm water they did not have the strength to chew, and once again they fell asleep.

Then Moyshe the wheelwright began to think of what to do, so that his family would not starve to death in their dark Odesa cellar home. He had nothing to work on or work with in Odesa. In the summer of the year 1921 he went to his wife's hometown, Khashchevate, so that her brothers in that small corner of the province could save his children from hunger-sleep.

And that was how Moyshe, the proletarian Jewish community councilman of Dubova, went from happy Jewish Odesa with its windows and doors open to the wide world, back into a scourged and plundered Jewish shtetl of the Podilia region to look for a new home for himself.

Odesa, Summer, 5680

Afterword

Cynthia Madansky

In 2020, I asked my father, Albert Madansky, if he would be willing to work with me on an English translation of a short Yiddish-language book entitled *Chronicle of a Dead City*, by Rokhl Faygnberg.

Although he was not a translator, but rather an acclaimed statistician, he was fluent in Yiddish and had translated some of the more obscure Sholem Aleichem stories for pleasure, as well as his father's, Harry/Hirschl (Zvi) Madansky, personal and polemic writings.

I was researching Yiddish women novelists for the third and final film in a trilogy about the Shoah and the "Jewish Question" (first two entitled *Past Perfect* and *E42*) and fell upon Faygnberg's only novel translated into English, *Strange Ways*. I was completely enamored by it. As I researched Faygnberg's biography and other writings, I came across *Chronicle of a Dead City* which seemed relevant to my future project, and which I hope to film, partly in Ukraine.

My father generously and eagerly agreed to partake in this *chevruta*, a Jewish study/discussion partnership, and for two years we met religiously for one hour each day (except on Shabbat) to work on the translation. I was in Brooklyn, he was in Chicago, and we were fully committed to our studying and translating Faygnberg's extraordinarily detailed retelling of the horrors of the pogroms that took place in the shtetl of Dubova, Ukraine.

We would take turns reading the original Yiddish text aloud, he would correct my pronunciation, and then reread the text so I could hear the cadences of the language. He would loosely translate the sentence, I would transcribe and then together we would compose and construct sentences, while engaging in discussions about the Yiddish language, sentence structure and syntax as well as Faygnberg's unique phrasing. Faygnberg's style was pragmatic, inflected with expressions of sarcasm—what my father termed an "insider's language"—a voice familiar to those who are fluent in Yiddish and Eastern European Jewish culture, history, and Judaism. He would remark on the references to the many Jewish rituals and prayers, the Torah, Mishnah, and Talmud. We had our many dictionaries by our sides to look up the Hebrew, Yiddish, German, Russian, and Ukrainian words, as well as Faygnberg's Hebrew edition of the text published in 1940 as a comparative text.

Our translation sessions were intense and rigorous, imbued with discussions, arguments, debates, and emotion. There were many moments that we had to take pause. Outside of our designated translation hour we often discussed the text, sharing essays, maps, film, and art about this very complicated and turbulent political period in Ukraine.

This *chevruta* with my father was not unfamiliar to me. It began during my yeshiva studies as a young child. At night, only after he could take a break from his own analytical work, he would call me to his study or we would sit at the kitchen table and he would help me with my homework, guiding me through Rashi, Talmud, Mishnah, and the Torah. We would read the texts in Hebrew and Aramaic, analyzing language, discussing meanings, cross-referencing interpretations, and I would not get up until he was convinced that I truly understood the meaning, for this was the foundation for the next day's texts.

This *chevruta* transpired across decades, discussing Jewish history, antisemitism, the state of Israel, nuclear war, grief, and trauma. It culminated (unknowingly at the time) in the translation of Faygnberg's book. My father's unexpected death came six months after we completed our work together.

Our translation was then brilliantly edited by Yankl Salant, who created a truly readable text which is ready to be shared with the public. Unfortunately, Albert was unable to read the final translation, but I know he would be as grateful to Yankl's work as I am.

We would like to thank Professor Elissa Bemporad, the Ungar Chair in East European Jewish History and the Holocaust and Professor of History at Queens College and the CUNY Graduate Center, for her encouragement in our undertaking of this translation project. Professor (Emeritus) Howard Aronson of the University of Chicago Departments of Slavic Languages and Literature and of Linguistics, and Professor (Emeritus) Moshe Taube, the Tamara and Saveli Grinberg Chair in Russian Studies of the Hebrew University of Jerusalem Departments of Linguistics and of Russian and East European Studies, who helped us translate some of the obscure Yiddish, Russian, and Ukrainian words in the text. Dr. Stella Hryniuk, retired Associate Professor of History, at the University of Manitoba, contributed by providing us with background on the political situation in Ukraine during 1919. We also thank Kim Kostyal, Michele Madansky, Paula Madansky, and Travis Mowbray for their reading of early versions of the translation. I want to also thank my dear friend Wendy Mills with whom I have been engaged in an ongoing *chevruta* with not only on this project, but on many other concepts and ideas for the last thirty years.

Lastly, during the years of working on this translation my mother Cara (Yore) Madansky, whose family is from Berdychiv, Ukraine passed away (August 2021) and six months after completing our last pass on the translation my father Albert Madansky died (December 2022).

This book is in honor of their memory.

September 1, 2024

NOTES

Introduction

1 For a comprehensive analysis of the events and the political responses to the trial and its aftermath, see David Engel, ed., *The Assassination of Symon Petliura and the Trial of Scholem Schwarzbard 1926–1927: A Selection of Documents*, Gottingen: Vandenhoeck & Ruprecht, 2016. See also Saul S. Friedman, *Pogromchik: The Assassination of Simon Petliura*, New York: Hart Publishing, 1976, and Kelly Johnson, "Sholem Schwarzbard: Biography of a Jewish Assassin," Doctoral diss., Harvard University, 2012.
2 On the contentious question of Petliura's responsibility in the pogroms, see for example, Christopher Gilley, "Beat the Jews, Save ... Ukraine: Antisemitic Violence and Ukrainian State-Building Projects, 1918–1920," in *The Pogroms of the Russian Civil War at 100: New Trends, New Sources*, Elissa Bemporad and Thomas Chopard (eds.), *Quest. Issues in Contemporary Jewish History*, no. 15, August 2019; Christopher Gilley, "Beyond Petliura: The Ukrainian National Movement and the 1919 Pogroms," *East European Jewish Affairs*, 47 (1) (2017): 45–61; Taras Hunczak, *Symon Petliura and the Jews: A Reappraisal*, Lviv: Ukrainian Historical Association, 2008; Volodymyr Serhiichuk, ed., *Pohromy v Ukraini: 1914–1920. Shtuchnykh stereotypiv do hirkoi pravdy, prykhovuvanoi v radiansk'ykh arkhivakh*, Kyiv: Vydavnytstvo imeni Oleny Telihy, 1999; and Serhii Iekelchyk, "Trahichna storinka Ukrainskoi revoliutsii: Symon Petliura ta ievreiski pohrom v Ukraini (1917–1920)," in Vasyl Mykhalchuk (ed.), *Symon Petliura ta Ukrainska natsionalna revoliutsiia*, Kyiv: Rada, 1995, pp. 165–217.
3 "France: Petlura Trial," *Time*, November 7, 1927, p. 1.
4 Ibid.

5 Engel, *The Assassination of Symon Petliura*, pp. 16, 54. Even the Soviet state, which was established after the end of the civil war, promoted the collection of personal statements and eyewitness accounts by victims and bystanders to the pogroms, and then dispatched the materials to the Paris judges to be used in the Schwarzbard trial. The Bolshevik motivation was solely political. By corroborating Petliura's liability in the anti-Jewish violence, the Soviet's forthright goal was to criminalize the Ukrainian forces that had fought against the Red Army during the civil war and thereby confirm the evil essence of Ukrainian nationalism. Perhaps also for this reason a rumor spread quickly among Ukrainian émigrés in France and elsewhere that Schwarzbard was in fact an agent of Moscow. While there is no evidence of Schwarzbard being a Soviet agent, the rumors might also have been supported by his short time in the Red Guard: in late 1917, Schwarzbard had briefly returned to Ukraine where he joined a Red Guard unit representing foreign anarchist elements and participated in the city's takeover by revolutionary forces in January 1918. He then returned to Paris. On the Soviet response to the Schwarzbard trial, see Elissa Bemporad, *Legacy of Blood: Jews, Pogroms, and Ritual Murder in the Lands of the Soviets*, New York: Oxford University Press, 2019, pp. 66–9.

6 "Acquittal of Sholom Schwartzbard is Condemnation of Pogroms," *Jewish Telegraphic Agency*, October 28, 1927.

7 On the Schwarzbard Defense Committee, its goals, and its membership, see Engel, *The Assassination of Symon Petliura* pp. 184–9.

8 Rokhl Faygnberg, *Pinkes fun a toyter shtot: khurbn Dubove*, Warsaw: Akhisefer, 1926. The Schwarzbard Defense Committee commissioned the French translation of the Yiddish original to the well-known French Jewish writer Moshe Twersky, who authored, among other works, the three-part novel cycle *L'Épopée de Ménaché Foïgel*. See Zalman Rejzen, "Rokhl Faygnberg (Imri)," *Leksikon fun der yidisher literatur, prese, un filologye*, Vilna: Kletskin, 1929, vol. 3, pp. 53–4.

9 Jews used the term *Lita* (in Hebrew) and *Lite* (in Yiddish) to identify the stretch of lands that were part of the former Grand Duchy of Lithuania, and included most territories of present-day Lithuania, Belarus, Latvia, as well as the northeastern regions of Poland.

10 For more information on Faygnberg's life and work, see also Sheva Zucker, "Rokhl Faygnberg (Imri)," *Shalvi/Hyman Encyclopedia of Jewish Women*, December 31, 1999. *Jewish Women's Archive*, http://jwa.org/encyclopedia/article/faygnberg-imri-rokhl (accessed February 18, 2024); E. Oyerbakh, ed., *Leksikon fun der nayer yidisher literatur*, vol. 7, New York, 1968, 343–6; Rachel Faygnberg, "Ayarati she-eynenah od," in S. Nachmani and N. Chonits (eds.), *Pinkas Slutsk u-vnoteha*, New York and Tel Aviv, 1962, 201–3; Faygnberg, "Ha-lyubanim le-beit imi," in ibid., 220–3; and Faygnberg, "Beit Nachum Epstein," in ibid., 223–4.

11 Rejzen, "Rokhl Faygnberg (Imri)," *Leksikon fun der Yidisher literatur*, p. 50.

12 Shomer was the pseudonym of Nokhem Meyer Shaykevitch (1849–1905), referred to by many of his critics as an author of *shund*, or trash literature, because of its frivolity and degrading moral character.

13 Rejzen, "Rokhl Faygnberg (Imri)," *Leksikon*, p. 51.

14 This autobiographical account was later published in book form as *Di kinder-yorn*, Warsaw: Hashakhar, 1909.

15 Rejzen, "Rokhl Faygnberg (Imri)," *Leksikon*, p. 52.

16 See Joanna Nalewajko-Kulikov, "'Her Way is the Future.' The Woman Question in Rachel Faygnberg's Journalism," *Polin: Studies in Polish Jewry* (2025) vol. 38; Elissa Bemporad, Joanna Degler Lisek, Francois Guesnet, and Antony Polonsky, eds., *Gender and the Body in East European Jewish History*, forthcoming, 2025. On why Jewish women's writings have been largely forgotten, see Anita Norich, "Translating and Teaching Yiddish Prose by Women," *In geveb*, April 2020. Available online: https://ingeveb.org/blog/translating-and-teaching-yiddish-prose-by-women (accessed September 28, 2024).

17 See Melech Ravitch, *Mayn leksikon*, vol. 1, Montreal, 1945, pp. 194–6.

18 Rejzen, "Rokhl Faygnberg (Imri)," *Leksikon*, p. 52. Her husband, G. Shapiro, a chemist, a relative of her mother's family, and twenty-five years her senior, passed away on the eve of the civil war.

19 David Kassel, ed., *Spektor-bukh*, Warsaw: Akhisefer, 1929, pp. 132–3. Translated by Elissa Bemporad and originally published in *Pakn Treger*, the Yiddish Book Center's English-language magazine.

20 Kassel, *Spektor-bukh*, pp. 132–3.
21 On the long history of anti-Jewish violence in Russia and Eastern Europe, see Eugene M. Avrutin and Elissa Bemporad, *Pogroms: A Documentary History*, New York: Oxford University Press, 2021.
22 On the Russian Imperial army's practice of branding Jews on the Eastern Front as dangerous "enemy aliens," which resulted in the expulsion and deportation of nearly half a million Jewish civilians, see Eric Lohr, "The Russian Army and the Jews: Mass Deportation, Hostages, and Violence during World War I," *The Russian Review*, 60 (3) (2001): 404–19; *Nationalizing the Russian Empire: The Campaign against Enemy Aliens during World War I*, Cambridge, MA: Harvard University Press, 2003; Polly Zavadivker, *A Nation of Refugees: World War I and Russia's Jews*, New York: Oxford University Press, 2024; and Semion Goldin, *The Russian Army and the Jewish Population, 1914–1917. Libel, Persecution, Reaction*, Cham: Palgrave Macmillan, 2022.
23 On recent scholarship on the pogroms of the civil war, see Jeffrey Veidlinger, *In the Midst of Civilized Europe: The Pogroms of 1918–1921 and the Onset of the Holocaust*, New York: Metropolitan Books, 2021; Elissa Bemporad, *Legacy of Blood: Jews, Pogroms, and Ritual Murder in the Lands of the Soviets*, New York: Oxford University Press, 2019; and Elissa Bemporad and Thomas Chopard, eds., *The Pogroms of the Russian Civil War at 100: New Trends, New Sources*, in *Quest. Issues in Contemporary Jewish History*, no. 15, August 2019.
24 On the myth of Judeo-Bolshevism, see Paul Hanebrink, *A Specter Haunting Europe: The Myth of Judeo-Bolshevism*, Cambridge, MA: Harvard University Press, 2018; and Bemporad, *Legacy of Blood*, pp. 1–34.
25 Kassel, *Spektor-bukh*, pp. 132–3.
26 Faygnberg wrote about the experiences and suffering of the Jewish refugees who fled the pogroms and were living on the Dniester river banks in the novel *Bay di bregn fun Dniester*, Warsaw: Tsentral, 1925.
27 On the massive scale of rape during the civil war compared to previous waves of anti-Jewish violence, see Irina Astashkevich, *Gendered Violence: Jewish Women in the Pogroms of 1917 to 1921*, Boston: Academic Studies Press, 2018; and Elissa Bemporad, "The Female Dimension of Pogrom Violence,"

in Eugene M. Avrutin and Elissa Bemporad, *Pogroms: A Documentary History*, New York: Oxford University Press, 2021, pp. 150–6.

28 The term *khurbn*, which means destruction or devastation in Yiddish and was used to describe major catastrophes in Jewish collective memory, including the destruction of the First and Second Temples in Jerusalem, was first employed by the writer and political activist S. An-sky in his diary-chronicle of the First World War, entitled *Khurbn Galitsye* (1921), the Destruction of Galicia. See Polly Zavadivker, *1915 Diary of S. A. An-sky: A Russian Jewish Writer at the Eastern Front*, Indianapolis: Indiana University Press, 2016.

29 On the rise of a *khurbn* research, or a unique genre of popular history writing that emerged in the wake of anti-Jewish violence during the First World War and the civil war, see Laura Jockusch, *Collect and Record! Jewish Holocaust Documentation in Early Postwar Europe*, New York: Oxford University Press, 2012; see in particular chapter 1.

30 Kassel, *Spektor-bukh*, pp. 132–3.

31 Elias Tcherikower ed., *In der tkufe fun revolutsye: memuarn, materyaln, dokumentn*, Berlin: Yidishe literarishe farlag, 1924, p. 1.

32 Towards the end of the civil war, Tcherikower relocated his archive, which he called Mizrakh yidisher historisher arkhiv, or the Archive of the History of Eastern European Jews, to Berlin. This archive, which played an important role in the Paris trial of Schwarzbard, is now located at YIVO in New York City. See YIVO Archives, Elias Tcherikower Collection, RG 80.

33 The Jewish Committee to Aid the Victims of the Pogroms (*Evreiskii obshchestvennyi komitet pomoshchi pogromliennykh*) or the Evobshchestkom was established as an aid organization in 1920 to provide welfare to pogrom victims and collect evidence of the violence and destruction.

34 On Kishinev, see Steven J. Zipperstein, *Pogrom: Kishinev and the Tilt of History*, New York: Liveright, 2018.

35 Rejzen, "Rokhl Faygnberg (Imri)," *Leksikon*, p. 53; while in Kishinev, Faygnberg published several accounts about the massacres in Ukraine for the Yiddish periodical *Der Yid*.

36 See David Roskies, *The Literature of Destruction: Jewish Responses to Catastrophe*, Philadelphia: Jewish Publication Society, 1989.
37 The *Memorbuch*, or book of remembrance, from the Latin "memoria," was a book used to commemorate the souls of those killed, and was used by the Jewish communities in central Europe, Germany in particular. The earliest one known was penned by the scribe Isaac ben Samuel of Meningen to commemorate the community of Nuremberg.
38 YIVO Archives, Elias Tcherikower Collection, RG 80, File 308, Folios 28936–29004, Rokhl Faygnberg, "Khurbn Dubove."
39 On Yizker bikher, see Jack Kugelmass and Jonathan Boyarin, trans. and eds., *From a Ruined Garden: The Memorial Books of Polish Jewry*, Bloomington: Indiana University Press, 1998; and Jennifer Rich, "Let This Book Be a Monument: Yizker Bikher and Jewish Collective Memory," in *Diaspora: A Journal of Transnational Studies*, 23 (2) (September 2023): 183–99.
40 The Russian translation was by prominent political and cultural historian Saul Ginzburg: Rakhil Faygnberg, *Letopis mertvogo goroda*, Leningrad: Priboi, 1928.
41 According to the 1897 census, there were 1,104 Jews living in Dubova. According to the data collected by the All-Ukrainian Relief Committee for the Victims of Pogroms and the Red Cross, 1,000 Jews lived in Dubova in 1918, and approximately 3,000 non-Jews, mostly Ukrainians. See Elias Heifetz, *The Slaughter of the Jews in the Ukraine*, New York: Thomas Seltzer, 1921, p. 341. In her account, Faygnberg noted that there were about 2,500 Jews and 1,050 non-Jews living in the town at the time, most likely inverting the numbers.
42 On Natan Hannover's *Yeven metsulah* (translated in English as Abyss of Despair), see Edward Fram, "Creating a Tale of Martyrdom in Tulczyn, 1648," in *Jewish History and Jewish Memory: Essays in Honor of Yosef Hayim Yerushalmi*, Elisheva Carlebach, John M. Efron, and David N. Myers (eds.), Hanover, NH: Brandeis University Press, 1998, pp. 89–112; and Adam Teller, "Jewish Literary Responses to the Events of 1648–1649 and the Creation of a Polish-Jewish Consciousness," in *Culture Front: Representing Jews in Eastern Europe*, Benjamin Nathans and Gabriella Safran (eds.), Philadelphia: University of Pennsylvania Press, 2008, pp. 17–45.

43 The Hebrew novelist Micha Yosef Berdyczewski, who spent his youth in Dubova, wrote about life in the shtetl in great detail and rather unsympathetically in a collection of short stories that he penned after he left. See Avner Holtzman, ed., *Mikha Yosef Berditsevski: Mehkarim u-te'udot*, Jerusalem: Am oved, 2002.
44 While a pogrom took place in Uman in 1905, in which three Jews were killed, no pogroms took place in Dubova in 1881–1882, nor in 1903–1905.
45 Not only does Faygnberg record the dates and times of the year according to the Hebrew calendar, but she also gives the chapter numbers in the original text in Hebrew letters.
46 The perpetrators buried the corpses of pogrom victims (and of some who were still alive) in the lime pits, thus robbing them of burial rites and individual graves. The lime pits also led to the rapid decomposition of bodies (which was in part a health measure to control the spread of epidemics). Hence, Moyshe the wheelwright mounted an act of resistance (unsuccessfully) by insisting that victims must be removed from the pits and buried according to Jewish law, before realizing that their bodies had decomposed beyond the point of recognition.
47 "The safe haven at that time was the lucky Jewish fortress of Holovanivsk, where a few hundred Jewish youth organized and armed themselves and would not allow any local or out-of-town bandits into the shtetl." On the understudied topic of Jewish self-defense during the pogroms of the civil war and its memory, see Mihaly Kalman, "Hero Shtetls: Jewish Armed Self-Defense from the Pale to Palestine, 1917–1970," PhD diss., Harvard University, 2017.
48 Faygnberg also recounts the episode of a young and beautiful Jewish woman who outwits the perpetrators by choosing to commit suicide instead of being raped. This is a leitmotiv that echoes through the memorial canon on anti-Jewish violence, including narratives of violence produced in the aftermath of the 1648 Khmelnytsky uprising or of previous waves of pogroms. Whether the episode about the young Jewish woman who outsmarted the rapers-to-be really happened or not is impossible to say.
49 Yehuda Bauer, *The Death of Shtetl*, New Haven and London: Yale University Press, 2009, p. 160. On the shtetl in the Soviet

Union (in Belarus in particular), see Arkady Zeltser, *Evrei v sovetskoi provintsii: Vitebsk i mestechki, 1917–1941*, Moscow: ROSSPEN, 2006; Leonid Smilovitsky, *Evrei v Turove: istoriia mestechka Mozyrskogo Polesiia*, Jerusalem: Tsur-Ot Press, 2008; and Albert Kaganovich, *The Long Life and Death of Jewish Rechitsa: A Community in Belarus, 1625–2000*, Madison: The University of Wisconsin Press, 2013. On Soviet ethnography of the shtetl and the economic collapse of the small market-towns, see Deborah Yalen, "'On the Social-Economic Front': The Polemics of Shtetl Research during the Stalin Revolution," in *Science in Context* 20 (2) (2007): 239–301; and Deborah Yalen, "After An-sky: I. M. Pulner and the Jewish Section of the State Museum of Ethnography in Leningrad," in Jeffrey Veidlinger, ed. *Going to the People: Jews and the Ethnographic Impulse*, Indianapolis: Indiana University Press, 2016, pp. 119–45.

50 A case in point is a recent study by Yehuda Bauer, in which the author examines the fate of the East European shtetl obliterated during the Holocaust. Bauer does remind us of the role played by the Bolshevik regime in destroying the shtetl in Soviet Belarus and Soviet Ukraine, forcing its Jews to migrate to larger cities in search of jobs. See Yehuda Bauer, *The Death of the Shtetl*, p. 5.

51 Faygnberg stayed in Odesa until December 1921, then crossed the border and moved first to Kishinev, then to Bucharest. She settled in Warsaw, but lived temporarily in Paris and in Mandate Palestine, where she eventually set up home in the 1930s. She published short stories and essays in *Haynt*, *Moment*, *Forverts*, *Der tog*, and even in the Bucharest *Manturea*. After settling in Mandate Palestine she mostly shifted to writing in Hebrew. Faygnberg died in Tel Aviv in 1972.

52 Rachel Faygnberg (Imri), *Megillat Dubovah: Toldot ir she-avrah u-vetelah min ha-olam*, Tel Aviv: 1940. Faygnberg kept contributing to the Hebrew-language press and published several works in Hebrew, including two novels, articles on Yiddish literature, and a five-volume series of sources titled *Megillot Yehudei Rusya: 1905–1964*, Jerusalem, 1965.

Text: Chronicle of a Dead City

1. Podvisote is a variation of Pidvysoke: Podwysokie, Podvysokoye, Podvysoke, Pidvisoke.
2. According to other sources, there were approximately 1,050 Jews and 3,000 non-Jews living in Dubova at the time. Faygnberg may have inverted the figures of the town's Jewish and non-Jewish population.
3. The first day of the Hebrew calendar year 5679 began on September 7, 1918 and ended on September 25, 1919. Faygnberg uses the Gregorian calendar year unless she is referring to incidents in Jewish communities, where she uses the Hebrew calendar year.
4. "Heder" is a traditional elementary Jewish school in which children are taught to read the Torah and other books in Hebrew. The heder's teacher was the melamed.
5. A "shochet" is a person officially licensed by rabbinic authority as slaughterer of animals and poultry for use as food in accordance with Jewish laws. The plural form of the word, which is "shochtim," appears a few lines down.
6. "Zemstvo" refers to the system of local self-government institutions whose jurisdiction included municipal economic, social, and educational affairs.
7. Alexander Kerensky was a Russian lawyer and a revolutionary who, following the February Revolution of 1917, led the Russian Provisional Government, a short-lived government that lasted until November 1917, when the Bolsheviks took over.
8. The term "Haskalah" refers to the Jewish enlightenment, a movement that became widespread over the course of the nineteenth century and promoted the acculturation of the Jewish minority into European society.
9. "Black Militia" refers to the Black Hundred, a reactionary, monarchist, and ultra-nationalist movement in Russia in the early twentieth century.
10. "Treyf" is defined as "ritually unclean or unfit according to Jewish law." It can also mean "non-kosher food" like pork. "Pig-treyf" here means "disgustingly unclean."
11. Mikha (or Micha) Yosef Berdyczewski (or Berditshevsky) would become a prominent writer. He wrote works in Hebrew, Yiddish, and German.

12 "Rebbetzin" is the wife of a rabbi.
13 *Katsap* is a Ukrainian pejorative term for Russians. It is the Russian word for "butcher" кацап. Going forward it will simply be translated as "Russian bastard."
14 The date of the fire Faygnberg is referring to is unknown.
15 Omtsenyu was the nickname of Avrom Ukelman.
16 It was the custom for members of the Jewish community to volunteer to provide meals on a specific day primarily for yeshiva students. This custom was referred to as *esn teg*, literally "eating days." That expression got shortened to *teg*, "days," as a descriptor of the meals.
17 The Duma, which constituted the lower house of the Russian Parliament, was an elective legislative body established by Tsar Nicholas II after the First Revolution of 1905. Four (and not three) Dumas were held between 1906 and 1917.
18 *Volostnoe zemstvo* means the local government council of the administrative subdivision. From here on we will use simply "volost."
19 The *Ispolkom*, literally executive committee, was an executive elected organ of soviets at all levels of state power. When Dubova came under Bolshevik control, Koretsky was elected to the Ispolkom of the city council of People's Deputies.
20 The Russians imposed a tax, called a *korobka* (box), to be paid by Jews for each animal slaughtered in accordance with Jewish law.
21 Wagon driver was among the humblest of the professions. Faygnberg may have been implying that this group was uneducated. Like other professions in the shtetl, wagon drivers too had their own minyan (literally, the quorum of ten adult Jews necessary for a formal religious service) or synagogue.
22 Faygnberg refers to Shkodnik as their "grandfather," even though he was their great uncle.
23 Faygnberg is referring here to the period following the Bolshevik Revolution of October 1917, when the Soviets established governing institutions in Dubova.
24 "Viddui" is a confession of sin recited privately by a person approaching death.
25 Kislev is the third month of the Jewish year, around December.
26 "Short Friday" refers to winter Fridays, when the sun sets earliest, giving Jews less time to prepare for Shabbos.

27 *Moskal* is generally considered to be a derogatory or condescending slur against ethnic Russians from Russia proper. The term is used by Ukrainians, Belarusians, and Poles in their respective countries. All further instances will be translated as Muscovite, which is equally derogatory.
28 Taras Hryhorovych Shevchenko 1814–1861 was a Ukrainian poet, writer, artist, public and political figure, who was convicted for promoting Ukrainian independence.
29 Ivan Gonta was one of the leaders of the Koliivshchyna, an armed rebellion of peasants and Ukrainian Cossacks against the Bar confederation in the Polish–Lithuanian Commonwealth. He led a pogrom in Uman in 1768.
30 1648 and 1649 the years of the Khmelnytsky massacres.
31 In 1648, Bogdan Khmelnytsky led the Zaporozhian Cossacks and local Ukrainian peasantry against the forces of the Polish–Lithuanian Commonwealth. During the uprising, the Cossacks committed mass atrocities against the Jewish population, killing as many as 10,000 Jews.
32 Symon Vasylyovych Petliura (1879–1926) was the Supreme Commander of the Ukrainian Army and the President of the Ukrainian People's Republic during Ukraine's short-lived sovereignty in 1918–1921, leading Ukraine's struggle for independence following the fall of the Russian Empire in 1917. He was assassinated in 1926 by the Ukrainian Jew Sholem Schwarzbard in retaliation for the pogroms carried out by the troops under his control.
33 The pogrom in Proskuriv that took place on February 15, 1919, and was led by Ivan Samosenko, constituted one of bloodiest massacres of the civil war. In just a few hours, over 1,600 Jews were murdered.
34 Several hundred Jews of Teplyk were murdered in July 1919 in a pogrom staged by the Ukrainian troops of Symon Petliura.
35 S. Shtogrin was a leader of the Ukrainian rebels against the Soviets, who was arrested and shot.
36 Numerous bands of partisans were formed at the time of the civil war. Red partisan detachments supported the Red Army against the White forces and the Ukrainian troops. Other partisan groups, especially those that sprang up in Ukraine, increasingly came to side with the national aspirations of the Ukrainian people, and eventually became the chief opponents of Bolshevik power in Ukraine.

37 The Ukrainian Socialist Revolutionary Party was one of the most influential political parties in Ukraine at the time. In 1918, it split into two factions. The Left SR favored the organization of an underground resistance and a cooperation with Bolshevik forces.
38 The Russian term *Zhid* is a derogatory word for Jew, analogous to the word "kike." We use Zhid as noun and (uncapitalized) zhid as adjective for all instances where Faygnberg indicates a pejorative reference to Jews.
39 Here "Black" refers to Nikolsky's support of the Black Hundreds, the reactionary and antisemitic league in Tsarist Russia, responsible for many pogroms.
40 Pesach Sheni is known as the "Second Passover" and is an opportunity for anyone who was unable to participate in Pesach the previous month to observe it. In 1919, it occurred on Wednesday, May 14, but, since according to the Jewish calendar, the day begins after sunset on the evening before the holiday, Faygnberg's reference to Tuesday is to the night preceding Pesach Sheni.
41 "Zhid authority" refers here to Soviet forces.
42 The opposition committee opposed the Soviets and the Revolution; "counterrevolutionary" is a term used by the Soviets themselves.
43 Fanye was Feyge-Vitele's nickname.
44 Ataman (or Otaman) was the official title of a military commander of the Cossack armies during the civil war. Symon Petliura, head of the army of the Ukrainian People's Republic, was called Supreme Otaman.
45 "Shiva" is the traditional seven-day period of mourning the death of a family member that is observed in Jewish homes. Observing this ritual is called "sitting shiva."
46 The Left SRs were a radical left-wing faction of the Socialist-Revolutionary party. Their members participated in the October Revolution and aligned with the Bolsheviks at the Second Congress of Soviets. The Left SRs were crushed by the Bolsheviks after a failed uprising in 1918.
47 May 15, 1919.
48 Referring to Kozakov, Smelnitski, and Kopnik.
49 Smelnitski and Kopnik.
50 Sivan is the third month in the Jewish calendar and usually falls in the months of May and June.

51 "Black Army" refers to the independent army led by Nestor Makhno, a Ukrainian anarchist revolutionary who fought primarily against the Bolsheviks and the White forces; they were named Black because of the color of the anarchist flag.
52 Anton Ivanovich Denikin was a Russian lieutenant general in the Imperial Russian Army (1916), who later served as the Deputy Supreme Ruler of Russia during the civil war. He was also the commander in chief of South Russia. When the Bolsheviks seized power, Denikin helped form the White Army to oppose them. Faygnberg's use of the words "black" and "Tatar" to describe Denikin in this sentence is derogatory. The same is true for the word "black" in the rest of the sentence, which refers to the counterrevolutionary stance of the White forces.
53 Faygnberg is mistaken about either the day or the date. The 20th of Sivan, 5679 began at sundown Wednesday, June 18, 1919, which means she refers to early morning of Thursday, June 19. The other possibility is she was correct in saying it was Tuesday early morning, which would make the Hebrew date the 18th of Sivan or June 17th, 1919.
54 June 18, 1919.
55 A revolutionary song named "Dubinushka."
56 On May 24, 1919, Kryve Ozero was attacked by a band of Ukrainians, who within several hours killed three hundred Jews.
57 These were atamans who led separate bandit groups that carried out pogroms in Uman.
58 Semi-official reactionary and antisemitic league in Tsarist Russia, responsible for many pogroms.
59 August 5–6, 1919 (sundown to sundown). Tisha b'Av is an annual fast day in Judaism, a commemoration of a number of disasters in Jewish history, primarily the destruction of both Solomon's Temple by the Neo-Babylonian Empire and the Second Temple by the Roman Empire in Jerusalem.
60 "Chuppah" is the wedding canopy, beneath which the Jewish wedding ceremony takes place.
61 A prayer in which one confesses one's sins accompanied by a beating of the chest.
62 A book of women's prayers in Yiddish.
63 The Saturday after Tisha b'Av, August 9, 1919.
64 From August 6, 1919 through the morning of the 9th.

65 It is not entirely clear what was meant here. The moniker "yidishe kapore" can mean "Jewish scapegoat" or "Jewish sacrifice," but since she was a Christian whose intentions were not always good, it could mean "sacrifice for the Jews" by way of revenge.
66 From the beginning of 1919 many pogroms were perpetrated under the name of the commander of the Ukrainian army Symon Petliura, either directly by his forces or by the peasant bands allied to him, particularly those led by Zeleny.
67 Reference to the fighting between the Red Army and the Directory of the Ukrainian People's Republic. As a result of the fighting, the Ukrainian army was forced to retreat from Kyiv and the government moved to Vinnytsia and in February 1919 came under the leadership of Petliura.
68 Kaddish, or Mourner's Kaddish, refers to the prayer traditionally recited in memory of the dead.
69 Title of what is popularly known as the "women's Bible," a Yiddish adaptation of many of the texts of the Bible.
70 The Hebrew month of Elul 5679 went from sundown of August 27 through sundown of September 25, 1919.
71 This is the Hebrew phrase referring to the prayer said for a deceased person at burial and at ceremonies in his or her memory. The phrase means "God of mercy."
72 The expression *a yidene a kozak* means "a domineering/enterprising Jewish woman."
73 In 1919 the holiday started on September 25.
74 In 1919 the holiday began on October 9.
75 Here Faygnberg is using "leper" as an insult for these Jewish traitors.
76 The All-Russian Extraordinary Commission, known as Cheka was the early Soviet secret police organization known for conducting the Red Terror.
77 The Great Synagogue of Odesa was also known as the Shalashna Street Synagogue.
78 In 1919 the month of Elul began on August 27 and ended on September 24.